La Place de la Concorde Suisse

JOHN McPHEE

La Place de la Concorde Suisse

Farrar / Straus / Giroux

NEW YORK

Copyright © *1983, 1984 by John McPhee*
All rights reserved
Printed in the United States of America
Published simultaneously in Canada by
Collins Publishers, Toronto
First printing, 1984
Library of Congress Cataloging in Publication Data
McPhee, John A.
La place de la concorde suisse.
UA800.M3   1984   355′.0330494   83–27466
The text of this book originally appeared in
The New Yorker and was developed with the editorial
counsel of William Shawn and C. P. Crow

For my daughters in their Wanderjahre

La Place de la Concorde Suisse

The Swiss have not fought a war for nearly five hundred years, and are determined to know how so as not to.

In Italy, it has been said of the Swiss Army, "I didn't know they had one." When the Italian learns that the Swiss Army vastly outnumbers Italy's, the Italian says, "That is not difficult."

The Swiss Army has served as a model for less languid nations. The Israeli Army is a copy of the Swiss Army.

Switzerland is two times the size of New Jersey. New Jersey, by far, has the larger population. Nonetheless, there are six hundred and fifty thousand people in the Swiss Army. At any given time, most of them are walking around in street clothes or in blue from the collar down. They are a civilian army, a trained and practiced militia, ever ready to mobilize. They serve for thirty years. All six hundred and fifty thousand are prepared to be present at mobilization points and battle stations in considerably less than forty-eight hours.

If you understand the New York Yacht Club, the Cosmos Club, the Metropolitan Club, the Century Club, the Piedmont Driving Club, you would understand the Swiss Army.

Some of these thoughts run through my mind as the Section de Renseignements—of the Eighth Battalion of the Fifth Regiment of the Tenth Mountain Division —gets ready to patrol a sector of the uppermost Rhone. The battalion has been told to move, and it is the business of these soldiers to learn as thoroughly and as rapidly as they can what their major needs to know about the new sector; for example, how many troops will fit in a cable car to the Riederalp? Where is a good site for a command post on the lower declivities of the alp above Lax? How many soldiers could sleep in the Schwarzenbach barn? Would that be all right with Schwarzenbach? Have explosives already been installed—as is the case at thousands of strategic points in Switzerland—to blow up the Nussbaum bridge?

With notebooks and pencils, the patrols of the Section de Renseignements go from place to place exploring, asking questions, collecting particulars, scribbling information, characterizing and describing people and scenes, doing reconnaissance of various terrains, doing surveillance of present activity, and tracking events of the recent past. Afterward, they trudge back and, under pressure of time, compress, arrange, and present what they have heard and seen. All of that is incorporated into the substance of the word "renseignements."

I have limitless empathy for the Section de Ren-

La Place de la Concorde Suisse

seignements. The leader of the second patrol today is Luc Massy, who entered the army ten years ago with essentially his present status. He is five feet eleven inches tall, with blond hair and an aquiline nose—trim, irreverent, thirty years old. The others are Jean-Bruno Wettstein, Denis Schyrr, Pierre Pera, Jean Reidenbach. Each wears boots, gaiters, a mountain jacket, and a woolly-earflap Finnish hat, and carries a fusil d'assaut, which can fire twenty-four bullets in eight seconds and, with added onomatopoeia, is also know as a Sturmgewehr. Massy wears hobnailed boots. Most of the other soldiers are younger, and when they came into the army were issued boots with rubber soles—Swiss crosses protruding from the soles in lieu of hobnails. Massy says he feels the north wind, and therefore the weather will be stable for three, six, or nine days. The air seems still to me—a clear and frosted morning at the end of October in a deep valley under Alps freshly dusted with snow. Using pocket calculators and topographic maps, the patrol has charted its assignments—uphill, down, up, down—figuring that eleven hours will be required to complete them. Accordingly, each man puts in his pack a plastic sack of lunch and a plastic sack of dinner—dried fruit, fresh fruit, bread, cheese, pâté, sausage, and bars that are labelled "Militärschokolade, Chocolat Militaire."

5

This is the Valais, the Swiss canton with the country's highest mountains—a canton divided by the west-running Rhone, which once flowed as ice five thousand feet deep to cut among the mountains its otherwise irrational groove. The Alps crowd the great chasm—off the left bank the Pennines, off the right bank the Bernese Oberland. The canton is divided in language as well, part French, part German, and not in a mixed-up manner, which would be utterly un-Swiss, but with a break that is clear in the march of towns—Champéry, Martigny, Sion, Sierre, Salgesch, Turtmann, Ausserberg, Brig—and clearer still in the names of the hanging valleys that come down among the peaks and plummet to the Rhone: Val de Bagnes, Val d'Hérens, Val d'Anniviers, Turtmanntal, Lötschental, Mattertal. The Tenth Mountain Division consists almost wholly of Suisses romands, as French-speaking Swiss are known. In their present exercises, they are well spread out through French and German Valais. In the German-speaking villages, soldiers puzzle at the names of streets and shops and understand nothing of the talk they overhear.

The divisionnaire of the Tenth Mountain Division is, of course, from French Switzerland—La Suisse Romande, also known as La Romandie. His name is Adrien Tschumy. On his shoulders—and nested in the fleece of his Finnish hat—are pairs of stars. There is a Swiss cross in the center of each star. The Divisionnaire is tall, trim, contemplative, with dark hair, a narrow face, and a manner that is quietly convincing. In military roles, the film actor Gregory Peck has resembled Tschumy, who resembles General MacArthur.

Tschumy must go to remote places to see his men in action. In Switzerland, there are no Fort Hoods, Fort Irwins, no vast terrains set aside for explosive games. There are few barracks. Troops on active duty for refresher courses (also known as repetition courses) are quartered for the most part in villages and towns, and if they are using live ammunition they must walk to far places to shoot. Here, for instance, Tschumy visits a company of grenadiers in the morning shadow of the Torrenthorn, six thousand feet above the Rhone. The Swiss Army grenadiers look upon themselves in the way that the United States Marines look upon themselves. The Swiss Army grenadiers specialize in events that take place at two thousand metres and skyward. They are technical climbers, schussbooming skiers, demolition experts, and crack shots, who sleep on granite mattresses and eat chocolate-coated nails. Some of them are bankers. Others are chauffeurs, dental technicians, civil engineers, alpine guides. They have discovered an enemy command post and are moving in its direction under the covering fire of automatic rifles. The bullets are bullets. Signal flags, understood all over Switzerland, have been set out to advertise the danger to passing promeneurs. Moving uphill, up a small cirque valley, the soldiers advance behind exploding grenades. Officers observe. One lieutenant works for I.B.M. in White Plains, New York, and has taken three weeks off to do his service. Crawling through snow under more bullets, the grenadiers reach the wall of the command post, a dotted line in their minds, and lay beside it a high-explosive plastic. They run. Chunks of broken rock rise out of the snow and fly in all directions, as much as three hundred metres—some above the head of the Divisionnaire. Like a theatre, the reverberant cirque enhances the explosion.

Meanwhile, certain boulders across a ravine have been identified as enemy helicopters that have just landed. For seven hundred years, Swiss soldiers have been masters of the mountain pass, and have looked upon the high divides not only as standpoints of invincible defense but as virtual weapons in themselves—terrain where the alien was disadvantaged and the Swiss could win battles even with falling rocks. Helicopters flout the mountain pass. The flying horses, as they are regarded, can appear from anywhere, come whirling over some unlikely arête, and with machine guns firing drop soldiers in the snow. The defense adapts. Men with bazookas on their backs run toward the helicopters and fall prone while their partners aim the tubes and fire. Explosions turn the choppers into scree.

Now the grenadiers discover the existence of an

enemy radio shack farther up the valley. They go after it with a blend of automatic rifles and grenades, crawling under the rifle fire to heave the grenades. The noise is loud to the point of pain, and the observing officers have fingers in their ears. Bullets rain on the mountain wall. The soldiers run forward, hide behind rocks. Grenades explode. As the soldiers move up the valley—now running low, now crawling, now inching along on their chests—a corporal walks upright behind them, like a football coach following the progress of a scrimmage. Wooden silhouettes representing enemy soldiers are blown and shot to bits. The objective is reached, and, with a final rush—with an explosion louder than any that has come before—the radio shack is taken without prisoners.

Walking back to lower ground, the Divisionnaire has many points to teach. Characteristically, he taps one index finger on the other as he talks. His primary point seems to be that the officers' preparation should have been more thorough. Intent on what he is saying, he does not look up. If he did, he could see out of Switzerland. He could see Mont Blanc, twice his altitude, bright in the morning light, and in Swiss terrain the Grand Combin, the Dent Blanche, the Weisshorn—a freshened sea of peaks beyond the deep airspace of the invisible Rhone. Resting level on rock and snow, a table has been set, with a red tablecloth; and the sun—at half past nine—has come over the Torrenthorn to shine on silver platters of rolled shaved beef, bacon, sausages, wedges of tomato, half-sliced pickles in the shape of fans. Officers stand around the table. There is a company of teacups in close ranks, another of stemmed glassware. There are baskets of bread. The wines are of the Valais. The red is Chapelle de Salquenen. The rosé is Œil de Perdrix, in a bucket full of snow. Tschumy drinks a cup of tea. A promeneur happens by—a citizen in knickers, boots, heavy socks, a mountain hat—on his way from who knows to where. He just appears, like a genie. His appearance suggests that he is above fifty and done with the army. He absorbs the scene: the festive table, the officers sipping and nibbling and quietly debriefing, the soldiers at a distance sitting in clusters on their packs, the charcoal streaks on the exploded snow. "Gut," he says, and he waves and walks on.

"Wiedersehen," the Divisionnaire calls after him, and the Divisionnaire is himself soon away—rising into the air in his Alouette III, his French six-seat jet-powered chopper, ascending among walls of red rock to cross into the Lötschental. Trending northeast, the valley rises toward the center of the Bernese Oberland. It is possible in Switzerland to be so far above and away from the Mittelland—the smooth perfected country that runs from Lake Geneva through Bern and Zurich—that even a Swiss valley, like the rough young mountains surrounding it, may seem penarctic and remote. The Lötschental is such a valley. The people of the Lötschental live in small, dark-cabin towns. A stream flows among them, pushing boulders. High serrated mountains are lined up in rows on either side, and the valley floor rises between them into fields of perennial snow. There are charcoal streaks on the snow. In the last five miles of the Lötschental, moving glacier ice is packed between the summits and leads to a gap where the converging mountains all but close. Twenty-five, twenty-six, twenty-seven hundred metres, the ice bends upward like the tip of a ski. Passing three thousand metres, the helicopter floats up a face of rock and moves through the gap into a world too bright for unshielded eyes. It is the top of the Bernese Oberland, where ice fields and snowfields are the white diameters of circumvallate arêtes, where all horizons are violent. The granite Jungfrau, the Mönch, the Eiger, the Fiescherhorn, the Aletschhorn, the Fiescher Gabelhorn conduct the eye across the glaciers to the gneisses of the Aar massif, to the obeliscal Finsteraarhorn, four thousand two hundred and seventy-three metres, the highest mountain north of the Rhone. Crystallizing and recrystallizing, the ice among the peaks collects and compacts itself into the Grosser Aletschgletscher, the supreme glacier of Europe, with avenues of ice coming in from six or eight directions to conjoin in a frozen intersection officially identified on maps as Konkordiaplatz, La Place de la Concorde Suisse. The Divisionnaire looks about him with a thoughtful smile. This place that will never need defending represents what the Swiss defend. In surroundings quieter than a jet-driven helicopter, I have heard him say that he is without reservation "persuadé de la valeur de l'effort de défense"—so thoroughly persuaded, in fact, that he gave up a career as a hydroelectric engineer to devote full time to the army. When he was a part-time artillery officer, rising to colonel, he was a civilian concerned primarily with the efficiency of turbines, which he understood so well that he practiced his trade not only in all parts of Switzerland but also from China to Chile to Hydro-Quebec. A couple of years ago, when he was fifty, he was invited to become an army professional.

The professionals are less than half of one per cent of the Swiss Army. They are not only officers but people of almost all ranks and specialties, who teach the militia the ways of war and help make the militia cohesive. Tschumy was given two stars for his hat and his epaulets, and responsibility for the Tenth Mountain Division. One star signifies a brigadier, and three stars a commandant de corps. There are seven commandants de corps, the highest-ranking officers in the army. The word "general" is not used except in situations of extreme emergency, when a fourth star is presented to one leader, chosen by the Federal Assembly.

In five centuries of neutrality, Switzerland has had four generals. The first was Guillaume-Henri Dufour, who was appointed in 1847 to suppress a rebellion of seven Catholic cantons: Lucerne, Uri, Schwyz, Unterwalden, Zug, Fribourg, and Valais. Neutrality does not exclude civil war. Dufour pounded the Catholics, who gave up after twenty-seven days. With paradoxical obscurity, his name rests on Dufourspitze, one of the least-known summits in the world, although it is the highest in Switzerland. Never mind that like the Matterhorn it is half Italian. Switzerland's other generals were appointed at times of nervous mobilization at the borders, of fearing what might happen as a result of proximate wars. General Hans Herzog became a national hero as the principal spectator of the Franco-Prussian War. In the First World War, General Ulrich Wille led the Swiss to victory. Victory consisted of successfully avoiding the conflict. As someone put it, "we won by having no war." In the Second World War, the victorious Swiss general was Henri Guisan, of the Canton de Vaud. There is a General Guisan Quai in Zurich, a Quai Général Guisan in Geneva. In every part of Switzerland, there are streets and plazas and equestrian statues—there are busts on plinths overhung with banners and flags—doing honor to the general of an army that did not fight. Switzerland defends itself on what it calls the Porcupine Principle. You roll up into a ball and brandish your quills. In the words of Divisionnaire Tschumy, "The foremost battle is to prevent war with a price of entry that is too high. You must understand that there is no difference between the Swiss people and the Swiss Army. There is no difference in will. Economic, military—it's the same thing. For seven hundred years, freedom has been the fundamental story of Switzerland, and we are not prepared to give it up now. We want to defend ourselves, which is not the same as fighting abroad. We want peace, but not under someone else's conditions. We will fight from the border. In response to a ground attack, which would in all likelihood come from the northeast, we intend to keep a maximum proportion of our land free. There are those who think we should train only for guerrilla warfare. That would be a form of giving up. Another possibility is that someone might use Switzerland by going through a corner or two, or to get to the north by the Simplon Pass or the pass of Grand-Saint-Bernard. We must stop that, too. We can really do something. We haven't enough tanks, but, given the nature of our terrain, we can fight with infantry. The first days of fighting would be dangerous for us. We would lose many people. But I am confident of our defenses. If I were not confident, I would not be a divisionnaire."

Like a fly inside a chandelier, the helicopter crosses

La Place de la Concorde Suisse. Making a shortcut to Alte Pür, it goes up the side of an arête, over the knife-edged rock, and crosses another glacier—the Fiescher-gletscher—under the spire of the Finsteraarhorn. It was below the Finsteraarhorn that the Swiss first figured out the movements and the sweeping implications of glacier ice, dominating a world that looked something like this. Wasenhorn, Firehorn, Chastelhorn—the mountains decline in altitude, the terrain falls toward the Rhone, whose valley, near its beginnings, is as narrow as the Lötschental and seems as remote. It contains two paved airstrips—but no airport, no evident hangars, no evident airplanes, no fuelling trucks, not even a wind sock. One sees such airstrips in many mountain valleys. Near the older ones are hangars that are rises in the ground. They are painted in camouflage and covered with living grass. Other strips are more enigmatic, since no apparent structures exist. If one just happens to be looking, though, one might see a mountain open—might see something like an enormous mousehole appear chimerically at the base of an alp. Out of the mountain comes a supersonic aircraft—a Tiger, a Mirage—bearing on its wings the national white cross. In a matter of seconds, it is climbing the air. Pilots sit inside the mountains waiting, night and day. On topographic maps revised and printed since the airstrips were built, the airstrips do not appear. The maps are sold in bookstores all over Switzerland, but those who wish to fill in the airstrips need their own renseignements. Even the map on the Divisionnaire's lap does not show the airstrips below. The Alouette crosses the Rhone, and goes south into the small, steep-sided Blinnental. It drops into the exact center of the V of the valley, and gradually to the floor, not much shy of the Blinnengletscher and the international divide. The Blinnental is essentially un-inhabited, and utterly so at Alte Pür—an alpine meadow, grazed some in summer, perhaps, but not extensively, and barren-looking now. It is a good place for artillery —a good place for forward observers to practice their art of defining the targets of the guns. Somewhere up a small valley on the north side of the Rhone is an obusier 46, which can throw fifteen kilograms ten kilometres and is practicing close to the limits of its range. The target is a cliff off the shoulder of an alp almost due south of the distant gun. Above the observers' heads, there is an occasional high hum, a soft whistle, as fifteen kilograms complete their parabola and zap the hapless alp. There is no concern whatever that if the shell should miss the alp it might go whistling into Italy. The shell is not going to miss. The observers are under camouflage nets with their field telephones and other equipment. Four such groups are in the meadow, practicing together on the same situation. Their major is Jacques Hentsch, and he says the shells are taking thirty seconds to reach the target from the gun. The observers compute the difference between the intended and the actual hit. On their telephones, they present the results to the artillerymen at the gun, who make the necessary adjustments and fire again. "No problem," says Major Hentsch. There is a problem, though. The calculations and the phone calls and the adjustments at the gun are supposed to take forty seconds, to which is added the thirty seconds of travel time for the ensuing shell. Now and again, a shell goes overhead and flame and thunder erupt from the alp, but not at anything approximating one-minute-and-ten-second intervals, and while the Divisionnaire—one index finger tapping against the other—speaks tensely to the observers Major Hentsch has leisure to remark that people in New York are indulging in pure hokum when they say that interest rates will continue to fall and thus the stock market is certain to go on rising. Nevertheless, he adds, New York is still one of the few places in the world where you can make money. Hentsch belongs to one of the most august and ancient private-banking families in Geneva. On his own, he has become well known for his resourceful development of new accounts. He manages portfolios. He says that he is like a priest, in that he must know his customers well in order to serve them. Less than a week ago, he was in Portland, Maine, buying lobsters. Last year, he bought twenty-five thousand lobsters, importing them through Zurich into Sweden. Of service in the Swiss Army, he says, "It belongs to the passport." And apropos of nothing at all he adds, "We are nice people. Not everyone understands that."

Why is the Divisionnaire so unhappy? With Swiss precision, every shell has exploded in an area smaller than the courtyard of the Pentagon, and the area is the target.

A communications problem, Hentsch explains, is causing the shells to come so slowly. The artillerymen at the gun are Suisses allemands, there being a shortage of artillery officers in La Suisse Romande. The forward observers are feeding back their data in French, which the people at the gun only poorly understand. The observers, for their part, observe nothing in German. The shells continue to come slowly. The shooting ends badly. A black soldier comes up to the Divisionnaire and offers him raclette for lunch. With grace, the invitation is declined.

When the Swiss Army maneuvers, the defending forces are designated blue and the enemy is red. In the Federal Assembly, the Communists complain. The Communists are one per cent, and the complaints are unavailing. This morning, as it happens, there is no enemy. The Section de Renseignements —of the Eighth Battalion of the Fifth Regiment of the Tenth Mountain Division—is collecting information from as yet uninvaded land. For Luc Massy's patrol, the starting point is the train station in Mörel, a village about seven kilometres up the Rhone from the Swiss end of the Simplon Tunnel. Sharing a bar of chocolate, the patrol is driven to Mörel in a Mercedes-Benz truck, winding through a steep country of orange tamaracks, isolated blazing maples, and the narrow cascading Rhone. "C'est loin! C'est loin!" Massy complains as each revolution of the wheels measures steps to be taken in return. Finally, as the truck noses downgrade and over railroad tracks, he says, "Voici la gare."

It is a one-metre railway, narrow-gauge and pri-
vately owned, known as the Furka-Oberalp. Four Haflingers—short and shaggy Austrian mountain horses—
graze by the station. In the Swiss Army, a Haflinger is a
small, tough four-wheel-drive vehicle. It is made in
Austria and looks like a cross between a mule and a jeep.
The téléphérique is near the station. There are two
routes, and the gondolas rise more than two and a half
kilometres to the shoulders of the Alps, connecting Mörel
to even smaller villages above.

While passengers—apparently farmers—patiently
wait, Jean-Bruno Wettstein interrogates the ticket seller.
The soldiers quickly compute. An entire company could
get to the top in fifty minutes.

The patrol moves out. Five hundred metres up the
river is the pont de Gifrisch. The patrol stands on the
bridge and carefully studies the river. Massy points.

"There is one."

"There is another."

"Three, four, five."

They are counting trout.

Their lieutenant pulls up in the Mercedes truck.
Instantly, they are alert to the features of the bridge. It
is a single span. It will carry twenty-eight tons. The
Rhone is flowing under it at three metres per second.

Last year, the lieutenant was studying at the University of Pennsylvania. His name is Olivier Wyssa. He
is from Geneva and has returned from America to practice law. He is a big man who wears light-sensitive eye-
glasses and has a mustache with short handlebars.

Lieutenant Wyssa moves on. The patrol leaves the
riverside and climbs the right bank a thousand vertical

feet. The actual distance does not seem a great deal longer to me, as I accompany them, or, I feel sure, to them, as they labor upward with packs and rifles. The rifles weigh six and a half kilos. The packs vary. Massy says, "We are supposed to get ourselves into condition before we go to the army, but we never do."

Jean-Bruno Wettstein smiles, and remarks, "In the Suisse Romande, we say, 'Why do we go to the army, anyway? There are always enough Swiss Germans to defend us.'"

In an experience that is characteristic of the alpine-valley country, the patrol comes to a road after climbing the thousand feet. It is a shelf in the mountainside, curving into reentrants and out around promontories. A major is waiting on the road. He is driving a Pinzgauer, which is—more or less—a large Haflinger, and is also named for a horse. The major is Guy Glauser. He manufactures dental equipment in Vevey. In the army, he is in charge of all intelligence in the Fifth Regiment, and therefore of all its Sections de Renseignements. He wants to know, among other things, if the pont de Gifrisch was mined.

The answer is negative. There would not seem to be a large point in blowing up a twenty-eight-ton bridge to prevent its being crossed by a fifty-ton tank.

Returning salutes, the Major departs. The soldiers walk the road. After a bend or two, they come upon a group of workers who are patching the surface. As the patrol goes by, a man in blue overalls touches the muzzle of Denis Schyrr's gun. Schyrr says, "He inserts the flower."

We are on our way to the Nussbaum bridge, via Göuchheit, Krizacher, and Vogelture—names that to these soldiers are neither native nor foreign. The patrol drifts along, for the moment making no notes—merely covering ground, telling stories.

There is a tale about the Swiss Foreign Minister at a reception in Paris in 1979, where a kindly gentleman introduced himself as "Pierre Mendès-France."

"Pierre Aubert, Suisse," said the Foreign Minister, amiably shaking hands.

There is litter—a paper cup, a plastic bag—at the edge of the road: a remarkable sight. "Are we still in Switzerland?" asks Wettstein.

We move in and out of meadow and forest, trees at sharp angles to the ground. Where the meadows stop, the line is distinct between the varying depths of green. From the Rhodes of Appenzell to the Canton de Vaud, there is a prototypical element in the Swiss rural scene: there is no sfumato; meadows are edged absolutely by dense, dark forest. Wettstein's profession has much to do with the expectable beauty of these reiterated land-scapes. He is an agronomist, thirty-two years old, and in winter he works at a Station Fédérale de Recherches Agronomiques, on an old estate near Nyon. In summer, he is out in the alpine meadows, which are his specialty and are not confined to the Alps. Many alpages, as the meadows are called, are rented by herdsmen from local communes, which own them. Farmers and their herds-men are not always assiduous about keeping the alpages in good condition and trim repair. Cattle wander into the trees, where they trample the forests threadbare, and that is most un-Swiss. Agronomists and others study the situation, decide what space should be for meadow and how much space should be for trees. The neat, absolute lines are drawn with subsidized fencing.

La Place de la Concorde Suisse

It is an incidental touch in the appearance of Switzerland, where human beings have coiffed nature at almost every altitude—accomplishing things with respect to the original that, truth be told, are rarely an affront. People who paint pictures that look like Switzerland are put down as simpleminded romantic idealists, whereas they actually belong to the literal-statement and compressed-rusticity school. It is possible that people who prefer landscapes without evidence of mankind have come to prefer them because evidence of mankind is ordinarily so disappointing. While making their artifacts everywhere attractive, the Swiss have not embarrassed their terrain.

If Switzerland is arguably the most beautifully developed landscape in the world, this is so, to some extent, through necessity, because Switzerland is so small; and its size creates a military problem, for Switzerland has much to hide. Thorn and rose, there is scarcely a scene in Switzerland that would not sell a calendar, and— valley after valley, mountain after mountain, village after village, page after page—there is scarcely a scene in Switzerland that is not ready to erupt in fire to repel an invasive war. "About this we don't talk," a colonel on the general staff said to me one day. "Don't ask me about it. But keep your eyes open. You may see something."

One does not have to be trained by the Central Intelligence Agency to see the airstrips like Band-Aids all over the Alps. There is no attempt to conceal them. No one is suggesting they are Autobahns that ran rapidly out of funds. Like the hangars within the mountains, further installations are more subtle. In forests are many clearings that seem to make no sense. On calendars, they would appear to be alpages. But there are no cows, no chalets, no herdsmen—and no one cuts a tree in Switzerland without a federal permit. Why, then, the patches of clear-cut woods? They are fields of fire. Hidden in the rock behind them are extremely modern cannons trained on something—the mouth of a tunnel, a pier of a bridge—that might need the instant attention of prepared fire. All calculations are long since logged, and the shells are ready to fly. Thousands of big guns are emplaced in the rock of Switzerland, and, to an extent that is secret, are continuously manned. On the road to Simplon Pass, above Brig—about ten kilometres from the sector of Massy's patrol—a new bridge stands on slim rectangular pillars more than four hundred feet above a wide gorge: a curving bridge, of white concrete with concealed suspension cables, lovely to behold, veering through space, an engineering masterwork. It has shortened and simplified the route over Simplon, and, Simplon being what it is, there can be no doubt that the Swiss are ready to dynamite the bridge at any moment, including this instant. The system of demolition is routinely practiced. Often, in such assignments, the civilian engineer who created the bridge will, in his capacity as a military officer, be given the task of planning its destruction. Once it is destroyed, it must stay destroyed, so there is need for covering fire. The Simplon road, traversing many cliffs, offers so much spectacle that people in automobiles tend not to study the stone in the retaining walls. It is block granite, or something like it, and in places the texture is a little off. One such place is two kilometres north of the high curving bridge. There is no stopping, no shoulder there beside the road, but if you pull off into the recesses of the next avalanche shed and walk back you see on close inspection that some of the granite is plastic. A couple of dozen plastic-granite blocks form two removable squares. In effect, they are windows—closed for the season. They look directly at the near end of the bridge. Prepared fire. "Don't ask me about that. But keep your eyes open. You may see something."

To interrupt the utility of bridges, tunnels, highways, railroads, Switzerland has established three thousand points of demolition. That is the number officially printed. It has been suggested to me that to approximate a true figure a reader ought to multiply by two. Where a highway bridge crosses a railroad, a segment of the bridge is programmed to drop on the railroad. Primacord fuses are built into the bridge. Hidden artillery is in place on either side, set to prevent the enemy from clearing or repairing the damage. All purposes included, concealed and stationary artillery probably number upward of twelve thousand guns. The Porcupine Principle. Near the German border of Switzerland, every railroad and highway tunnel has been prepared to pinch shut explosively. Nearby mountains have been made so porous that whole divisions can fit inside them. There are weapons and soldiers under barns. There are cannons inside pretty houses. Where Swiss highways happen to run on narrow ground between the edges of lakes and the bottoms of cliffs, man-made rockslides are ready to slide.

Through locked gates you see corridors in the sides of mountains—going on and on into the rock, with a light in the ceiling every five metres and far too many to count. There are general hospitals inside mountain rock. There is stored petroleum—at least enough to fuel the completely mobilized army for more than a year, from the first jet aircraft to the last Haflinger. There is food, of course, and, needless to add, munitions. All these things have shelf lives and are regularly sold or otherwise used, while fresh materials are added. There is a Swiss Army bread that lasts two years. It is vacuum-packed and hard as rock. When exposed to air, it swells and softens. Munitions are hidden also in forests. Captains know where they are.

Various countries spy on Swiss defenses and attempt to diagram the hidden installations—including the Soviet Union, whose mapping project in Switzerland has not escaped the notice of the Swiss. The Russians obviously regard armed neutrality as a charming paper phrase. They associate Switzerland with the North Atlantic Treaty Organization, even if Switzerland protestingly does not. The Russians appear to look upon Switzerland as a kind of capitalist Alamo—a likely position of ultimate defense for a falling Western Europe.

Riding around Switzerland with these matters in mind—seeing little driveways that blank out in mountain walls, cavern entrances like dark spots under mountain-side railroads and winding corniches, portals in various forms of lithic disguise—you can find it difficult not to imagine that almost anything is a military deception, masking a hidden installation. You see the big closed doors of a building that appears to be a garage for snow-plows. But why would snowplows need to be surrounded by such a high fence and so much barbed wire? Possibly they plow snow with ten-and-a-half-centimetre cannons. Possibly the building is something like the top of a mine shaft. Not all underground installations are entered

24

through the sides of mountains. Some are entered through ordinary buildings and basements—and spread out far underground. You see a mountain, quite able to retain its own sides, with a huge wall of concrete set into its base, apparently doorless, windowless—blank. Elsewhere, you see talus, and when you look up to see the mountain that shed it there is no mountain. You infer that such material came from somewhere, and sense the vastness of underground spaces by the volume of the broken rock.

There are three defense centers, each almost wholly concealed, that are known as fortresses—one near the Austrian frontier, another at the head of Lake Geneva, and the third in the region of Saint Gotthard, the central Alpine pass. The fortresses have been likened to underground ant colonies, and they are continuously manned. While soldiers like Massy and Wettstein patrol the valleys and the hills to satisfy refresher courses, others in the militia spend the same time underground. The fortresses are somewhat misnamed—Festungen, forteresses—for the word seems to imply a unitary citadel, a Fort Ticonderoga by the shore of Lake Champlain, when in fact the fortresses are networks of tunnels, caverns, bunkers, and surface installations, each spread through many tens of square miles. Supplementing the fortresses is a much more widely distributed system of redoubts—rock-defended installations of related character, some of even greater size. The dimensions, sites, and purposes of all these defenses are secret even within the army—known only to those who need to know. Ironically, some of them were built with the help of foreign workers, who know where they are, while Swiss do not.

Switzerland seems to be ready for any invader—red, black, yellow, or white.

"We are going to be neutral, and whoever wants to come in here and make use of our territory, in action against us or a third state, we will kick him out."

"It's not playing, what we do."

"We are quite ready. The basic Christian idea is: I smash you; you turn and say, 'Smash here also.' The Swiss are not going to do that."

"In the Second World War, the will to defend was absolutely there. That will is very much unbroken."

The speakers are Swiss colonels, majors, and captains. The dialogue consists of fragments assembled from visits here and there.

"In Switzerland, there are people prepared to fight even against the government if the government were to capitulate."

"We dislike war. We don't want war. We must be

so impressive that the war never starts. I'm not sure we can do that. But I hope we can."

"Ten per cent of the people of Switzerland are in the Swiss Army. If ten per cent of the people in the United States were in a Volks army, it would include twenty-two million personnel. Think of the impression *that* would make on the Russians. An army is always a matter of impression, isn't it?"

"Even if we are subjected to nuclear blackmail, we will never give up."

Within all these remarks lies the essential nuance of the Swiss idea of neutrality—the essential nuance being brute military power. The Swiss definition of neutrality absolutely includes an army, because the task of a neutral country is to defend its territory. Switzerland's declaration of independence is that it will attack no one, will participate in no so-called police action, will make no alliance, and will defend itself. In a book subtitled "La Suisse en Armes" is a picture of a small boy beside a large cannon under a camouflage net, with the caption "Pour rester libre, un peuple libre a besoin de canons." Bumper stickers on Swiss cars say:

TOUS PARLENT AU SUJET DE LA PAIX
NOTRE ARMÉE L'A PRÉSERVÉE

"You have to be strong defensively to be neutral. Our population density and our terrain make armed neutrality possible."

"You need trumps, and the Alpine passes are our trumps."

"The Swedish are as aggressively neutral as we are.

27

They spend a lot of money on their army. But they have a lot of land. It is doubtful that they could defend it."

"Japan could do it. But they have too many people. with a hundred and seventeen million people, they will soon fall off the islands. And then what will they do? They will spread out into the Pacific again."

Switzerland—sixty per cent alpine—has a fistful of trumps. And altogether the Swiss national periphery is a natural defense. The high Alps, of course, form the southern and eastern frontiers, while the northern and western borders are largely defined by the Jura—a range of older and gentler mountains—and by two considerable lakes: Lake Geneva, also known as Lac Léman, and Lake Constance, the Bodensee. The Jura is so thoroughly prepared that it suggests a beached and camouflaged battleship. While attack could come from anywhere, it is anticipated from the northeast. When an officer sketches a map of basic national strategy, like as not he will draw an arrow coming in from that direction, and he might say, "That is the main assumption. Because we are neutral, we are not allowed to say that—but that is the assumption."

Within its natural shell, the army's initial mode of defense is to make clear that anyone who wants to travel aggressively through central Europe might find it advisable to avoid Switzerland.

"The invader sees the type of army we have, the density of the troops—and decides it is not worthwhile to invade. Then we have done something."

If deterrence fails, the border country is defended everywhere by contiguous embunkered brigades—soldiers in the thirty-three-to-forty-two age group who regularly train in the same places and collectively know every tree. There is some debate about Basel. It is Switzerland's second-largest city, and an industrial treasure, but it lies beyond the Jura—so close to Germany that one of its railway stations is a part of the German rail network, and passengers have to go through German customs in order to board a train, and so close to France that people at one chemical and pharmaceutical firm (Sandoz) have to go through French customs to get to the company tennis courts. How is anybody going to defend that?

"In the center of Basel, you can defend a few houses; otherwise, forget it."

"You can blow up the Rhine bridges. That's about all. Basel could not be defended."

"While Lake Geneva, the Alps, Lake Constance, the Rhine, and the Jura circumscribe Switzerland, Basel is out in the cold."

"Basel? Undefendable? Just try coming in here. You don't want to come into a town like this with a mechanical army. It would be rather nasty."

Given Basel's apparent vulnerability, it is worthy of note that the army is constantly there. The army is not conceding an inch of Switzerland. In the rush-hour twilight of a November day, I was walking across the Rhine on the Mittlere Brücke when half a dozen soldiers in combat camouflage ran onto the bridge with a very long wire and inserted it in a hole. From time to time, a head popped up through the hole. Passersby scarcely seemed to notice all this. Bridge-blowing practice is quite routine in Basel.

After the enemy seizes Basel, and overwhelms or bypasses the defenders of the Jura, the next several lines of resistance have been drawn in the Mittelland. Lying between mountains, the rectangular center of Switzerland is as rich as a chocolate bar and about as easily consumed. In a nation renowned as dairyland, it is the creamiest country that God has ever seen. It is the billowing, stream-dissected plateau country of Gruyère, of the Emmental, of the Lake of the Four Forest Cantons. It contains most of the Swiss population, most of the nation's wealth and industry. It contains Bern, Lucerne, Zurich, Winterthur. Switzerland has three entire army corps in the Mittelland alone. The corps de campagne, as they are known, consist almost wholly of élite troops, which is to say young ones. Strategically, to slow an enemy there is not much to blow up in the Mittelland; but the corps de campagne are highly mobile, mechanized, flexible, and extensively practiced in flame-throwing, grenade-tossing, bullet-spattering house-to-house combat.

"The price for a Russian invader is quite high. Even the Mittelland is bad for mechanized troops—so many houses, towns, rivers, so much population density. The topography is vulnerable, but the civil infrastructure is a defense in itself. You can't fight a big mechanized battle there."

The Mittelland is nevertheless about as vulnerable as Basel. And it presents a strategic paradox. The army is better off in the mountains. The people are better off with the army. During the Second World War, when the planned strategy was to leave the Mittelland open and defend the Alps, many citizens of the Mittelland spent the war in the mountains. The strategy now is to defend the Mittelland with troops that are prepared and equipped to pull back rapidly into the Alps. There are

at present no plans for withdrawing the civilian population to the mountains, but in significant numbers that
would certainly happen.

"The army can't very well defend mountains and
leave people behind."

In July of 1940, when General Guisan convoked
his commandants on the meadow where Switzerland, in
1291, was formed, he spoke of "the natural force of our
country, the incomparable possibilities for resistance offered to us by our terrain, rich in obstacles and cover,
our mountains above all." He called the Alps invincible,
and the people who have succeeded him echo what he
said.

"We are sure we have a fair chance, because of the
specialities of our country. We can easily block an
attack. Where there are not mountains, there is water on
every side. Someone who attacks us has to cross it. We
have a very strong infrastructure in the mountains. We
have a good chance that no one will attack us, because
the price he has to pay is too high."

"The Alps are younger and less eroded than, say,
the Rocky Mountains. There is less level ground among
them. Thus, they are an even greater obstacle."

"In the mountains, mechanization doesn't help you
any. You are almost lost with armored cars."

"The Gotthard freeway can be protected by ten
men. This is exactly what you see in Afghanistan. The
Russians cannot deal with that except by getting out of
their armored cars."

If the enemy were to come into the Alps, they
would encounter still another army corps—including
Soldat Wettstein, Soldat Massy, Lieutenant Wyssa, Ma-

jor Hentsch, Divisionnaire Tschumy, and the Tenth Mountain Division. In rough outline, the idea in the mountains is to blow up every point of access to the regional fortresses, so that armed forces—friendly or hostile—can go in and out only by helicopter. Needless to say, the demolition is ready.

"Don't forget: this is not the Plain of the Schleswig-Holstein. Our terrain is prepared for destruction, and then it defends itself."

And what if it does not?

"Our lines of defense are deep—one, two, three, four, five, six, seven. If all lines are penetrated, if the enemy comes into the Alps, guerrilla warfare follows."

And what then? Perhaps it would be apposite to ask a foreign military strategist rather than a Swiss—Switzerland's defenses being less than unknown to people in other armies.

"I personally would hate to have to go in there and dig them out. It would take a tremendous amount of force to peel them out of those god-damned mountains. For anyone who wants to go in there, the cost would be very high; and it would be even more expensive to stay in. They all know how to shoot, and shoot well. They would fight tooth and nail. They know their country like the back of their hand. And remember: theirs is a different mission from ours or most armies'. They do not have to be trained to fight in deserts or malarial swamps, to chase an enemy out of one physiographic world and into another. Their mission is to defend Switzerland. It is all defensive. They are a strong armed force —amazingly well trained for a country that hasn't been in a war for hundreds of years."

Luc Massy shifts his rifle on its strap and ventilates himself by unsnapping his jacket. "If war came, I don't think we would resist very long," he says. "But the army is very good for unemployment. When the army comes, many people in the villages are working."

"To defend Switzerland from the mountains is a myth," Jean-Bruno Wettstein says. "No enemy will come into the Alps. The population is in the Mittelland, and we have nothing to defend here but rocks, snow, and téléphériques. As a soldier, as a citizen, I really don't understand the possibilities of the Swiss Army. Given what I know of other countries and their armies, I don't think we can defend Switzerland."

"We may not have a very big chance, but as long as we have a small chance it is useful to do it," says Massy.

Wettstein replies, "If you put ten divisions of Russian

tanks in Basel, they won't take too much time to arrive in Geneva."

The patrol has walked several kilometres on the high ground above the Rhone and now looks down on the Nussbaum bridge. The drop is steep at first, through a meadowful of agile cows, and then considerably steeper. Massy, chef de patrouille, cannot see a way to go down, and neither can anyone else. Massy looks west, studying possibilities. Massy looks east. Massy looks down at his boots and past his toes to the Nussbaum bridge. What to do? The hour is somewhat past noon. The sun at last is bathing the deep narrow valley. The breeze is becoming warm. The larches are bright gold. The meadow is dry. The bridge can wait. When in doubt, eat lunch.

We sit down and break out our Valais bread and cheese. Across the valley, a waterfall erupts from dark wooded slopes of the Bettmeralp, which is treeless and white far above. Near the waterfall, a dark-brown village clings to the alp. Over our heads, an eagle is sliding through the sky. Massy removes from his pack a bulky towel and unrolls it to reveal a bottle of wine. In his battle jacket he keeps a tire-bouchon, always ready, like a grenade. He opens its knife blade and deroofs the leaded wine. He erects the corkscrew and revolves it into the cork. He sets the lever arm on the lip of the bottle. We hear the sound of a tennis ball, well hit. Massy runs the cork by his nose. In his breast pocket, at all times, is a small plastic cylinder that resembles a dice cup. It protects a drinking glass so small that even in its sheath it does not create a bulge in the jacket. With straight, converging sides, it has the simple shape of a peach basket, if not the size. It holds six centilitres and is a verre de cave, a winemaker's glass, whose proportions any Swiss winemaker could identify as the glass of the Canton de Vaud.

Massy fills the glass, holds it up to his eye. "Santé," he says, with a nod to the rest of us, and—thoughtfully, unhurriedly—drinks it himself. Because I happen to be sitting beside him on his left, he says, "John, you are not very well placed. In my town, we drink counterclockwise." After finishing the glass, he fills it again and hands it to his right—to Jean Reidenbach. The background music is a dissonance of cattle bells. We count nineteen Brown Swiss in the meadow just below us, and they sound like the Salvation Army. A narrow red train appears far below. Coming out of a tunnel, it crosses a bridge, whistling—three cars in all, the Furka-Oberalp. The train will go up the Rhone until there is no more Rhone, and then climb on cogs to the Furka Pass, and the Oberalp Pass, to finish its journey descending the nascent Rhine, pool to cascade pool, pastel green with glacial flour. The railroad bridge is a beautiful stonework that looks like a piece of a cloister. In all respects but width, it shames the Nussbaum bridge, the latter being wide enough for two automobiles or possibly one red tank. A téléphérique is down there as well. We are too high to see trout. Wires go up the Bettmeralp. Denis Schyrr volunteers to get the necessary facts at the téléphérique station later on, but he adds, "Do you suppose they speak French?"

Massy shrugs. He takes the glass from Reidenbach, refills it, and hands it to Schyrr. "This is a good way to drink," Massy remarks. "A good way to avoid getting —you know—drunk." Six centilitres is about two ounces. If the glass were filled with whiskey, you would know you'd had a drink. The apples and sausages are fresh and good, less so the pâté in the can. The sunlight is delicious. The packs are supportive. The rifles lean against a tree. After Pierre Pera, it is my turn to drink, and then Massy's, Reidenbach's, Schyrr's, Wettstein's, Pera's, mine, and Massy's. Pera is a plumber in Montreux. Denis Schyrr, blond and scholarly with his metal-rimmed spectacles, is a landscape gardener, a paysagiste-horticulteur, in La Tour de Peilz, near Vevey. Jean Reidenbach, with his tall rustic frame and unruly hair, looks like some sort of paysagiste himself, but is in fact a receptionist at the Ramada in Geneva. The wine is light and pleasant, not to say elegant. Massy pours himself another measure and contemplates it against the Bettmeralp, gold on white. From the one bottle, it is amazing how many times the glass will go around. It stops where it stops—even if the ritual ends, as it always begins, with Massy. Fraternité—yes. Égalité—no. Last month in Lausanne, at the Concours de Jean-Louis, Massy placed sixth in a field of ten thousand wine tasters. Here in this Valais meadow, the label on the bottle in his hand says "Clos du Boux, Epesses. J.-F. Massy, Propriétaire." J.-F. is Massy's father, now his partner, who is trim, compact, has an aquiline nose, and—including the bemused smile —looks exactly like Massy. Also on the label is a line drawing of a two-story house with a Bernese roof, Lombardy poplars at each end. It is completely surrounded by the vines of the Clos du Boux. The house consists of two ground floors, affixed to the slanting vineyard. Massy lives downstairs with his wife and infant son. His father and his mother live above. He leans on his pack and in the balmy sunlight closes his eyes. Three days ago, he was in Epesses making wine.

The cave was a ganglion
of hoses and tubes: Massy fixing leaks with surgical
cotton, Massy on a ladder with a light bulb and a cord,
Massy inside the cuves. He was wearing high rubber
boots, bluejeans, and a rubber apron over a cotton football shirt bearing the number "26" and the name
"BROWNS." He was racking a new white—in its taste a
hint of something foul. Time had come to separate the
wine from its lees. The ladder was leaning against the
tiled wall of a cuve—a tall and narrow chamber full of
wine. On the outside of the cuve, a column of wine in a
clear-plastic tube reported the depth inside. In this cave
were twenty-one cuves, also a big oak cask—in all, a
hundred and thirty-five thousand litres of wine. Massy
was working alone. He was working like a soldier. With
a hose that could have put out a fire, he sent most of the
contents of a cuve into an aeration tub, where it spilled
like a fountain into a foaming pool and by another hose
was sucked away. The wine was not at all attractive. It

looked like floodwater, like weak tea with skim milk in it, like something a chemical company had decided to hide. Sometimes he was interrupted by people who came to the cave to buy the product from the oenologist himself. Between rackings, he might have a few moments to sit and read *La Tribune du Matin*, but scarcely enough time to turn a page. He was racking at the rate of thirty-two thousand litres a day. Now and again, he picked up something that looked like a flamethrower and shot needles of cold water with steamlike force over the walls and floor of the cave. "If you are clean—if everything that touches the wine is clean—it is easy to make wine," he said. From time to time, he would pick up a small hose and let a slow downbending stream of wine fall past his tongue until he found the moment where the quality stopped. When a cuve was drawn down and its wine transferred, he opened a small oak door at the bottom and mucked out the offensive lees. They came forth like a warm coffee ice cream that had begun to sour. Putting on a yellow rain slicker, an impermeable yellow hat, Massy then crawled inside the cuve. If odor could kill, he would have fallen dead. He hosed out the interior. This had been a most unusual year, he said from inside —his voice distorted, tympanic, echoing, fermenting. He said he would be making about a hundred and seventy thousand litres—a volume approaching twice his annual average. There had been a fine spring, a better summer, with ample but not excessive rain. "Also," he added, "for four years the vines have not given much."

The door of the cuve was so small that a larger man could not have gone through it. It had the circumference of an oval placemat. After Massy came out, he lined the edges with beeswax, replaced the oak, and tried to secure it with a bolt. He had repeated trouble with the thread of the bolt. Minutes went by while he could not make it tight. "Losing time!" he shouted out in his frustration. "Losing time for Massy! Merde!" The soldier who would soon be joking in the mountains was someone else in the cave.

The cave was the basement of a building with thick stone walls, tall oak doors, and blue shutters, on the main thoroughfare of Epesses, a street so intimate that red and green lights forced the traffic to move in one direction at a time. Epesses was the sort of town that could stop a tour bus like a cork in a bottle. Two bicycles would have had difficulty passing in the Ruelle du Vieux Bourg, where the facing eaves of houses all but touched. On the walls there, and all over town, were grapevines and ivy, geraniums and roses, in vigorous color so late in the fall. Springwater poured into stone fountains from spigots set in the walls. Three hundred and sixty people live in Epesses, and if they step outdoors they are leaving town. All around the village are paths among the grapes. The paths run between stone walls and are decorated with stern advice: "DÉFENSE DE PRENDRE DU RAISIN." Also between stone walls, a small stream tumbles into town, passes through Massy's winery, and falls white and cascading to Lac Léman. The vineyards, leaning back from the water, collect the African sun.

Just the one house—Massy's, with its four chimneys (each with a tiled roof), its oak timbers, its balcony of beams and posts—stands apart from the town, suggesting a certain preeminence. It has been there for three hundred years, a long curving structure convex to the view

—across the village rooftops to the lake far below and the Savoy Alps beyond. Epesses is the ancestral village of Divisionnaire Tschumy. It is the village also of Eric Dessemontet, a vintner who has achieved the rank of captain and commands the company in which Massy serves. Vineyards are measured in fossoriers—an ancient reckoning of the amount of ground that could be worked by one man in a day. In the Lavaux wine region, of which Epesses is a part, an average winemaking family has thirty fossoriers. Dessemontet has twenty-eight. The Massys have a hundred and seventy. Protestant refugees, they came to Switzerland from France when the Edict of Nantes was revoked. They made watches for a time, and then wine. They have been soldiers for centuries, too, and now, despite the pressures of the great vendange, it was time for Luc to hang up his hoses and get out his gun.

In the trunk of his white Lancia he put his automatic rifle, his sealed container of bullets, his steel helmet, his various bottles of vin militaire. The football shirt disappeared and was replaced by his dress uniform, in Switzerland's dark sea green. That Swiss soldiers keep weapons and bullets and gas masks at home is one of the open details of rapid mobilization—a procedure that is for the most part classified. To the elemental question "Is your army ready to fight?" a member of the Swiss Army general staff will quickly answer, "Oh, yes, and we don't want to talk about that." All soldiers know their mobilization points and have been told not to reveal where they are. They have been told to go there by any means—on foot, if necessary. If they stop passing cars, the drivers transport them. The soldiers are supposed to carry food and drink for two days. In 1977, a

Swiss brigadier (one star) was sent to prison for eighteen years for giving secrets of mobilization to the Russians. Mobilization begins with an invisible process whereby certain strategic components normally found in concentration are systematically spread out. Partial mobilization, being more difficult than general mobilization, is more frequently practiced. In either situation, soldiers go from mobilization points to assembly areas to alert or battle positions.

All in forty-eight hours?

"That is rather long. If we start in the morning, we would be mobilized by late afternoon. That is why the gun is at home, the ammunition at home. The younger people all have automatic rifles. They are ready to fight."

In the thirteenth century, the confederating peasants kept their weapons at home. The sword became a symbol of their right to vote. In Appenzell, men still carry swords when they turn out to vote.

There are six hundred thousand assault rifles in Swiss homes. It is said that this is a very good thing, for while a father cleans his rifle at the kitchen table his son is watching, and "the boy gets close to the weapon." Communist Swiss soldiers keep rifles and machine guns at home. It is said that this is not dangerous for political purposes; it is dangerous only for the wife. Ammunition boxes are sealed. If the seal is not intact when a soldier returns to duty, serious punishment follows.

On Swiss highways, portable blinking signs appear from time to time, showing certain truck drivers where to turn and go in practice mobilization. When a Swiss citizen buys a truck, the registration may carry a notice that the truck will be taken over by the government in

41

time of war. Not all Swiss trucks are included—just the percentage needed. The owners have no choice.

After a last look around the cave and a chat of farewell with his family, Massy got into his Lancia and drove east on the Route du Vignoble—La Corniche de Lavaux —from village to village halfway up the lake slope, with tens of thousands of vines below him and tens of thousands above, terraced by retaining walls. He said the underlying rock was limestone, forever feeding nutrients to the soil. He said the reflection coming off the lake is particularly strong around Epesses and is known as the second sun. The retaining walls are unusually high, and they keep the sun's heat and warm the vines at night. "The berries go on ripening even in the dark."

On a street in Montreux, he picked up Gilles Fantony, a friend he sees only in the army. An ordinary soldier, like Massy, Fantony is the Swiss equivalent of a stockbroker, employed by the Union Bank of Switzerland. Over the past three weeks, he had grown a beard, so that he would not have to shave while in the army.

The Lancia proceeded along the lakeshore, and at Chillon the road became confined to an extremely narrow space between a cliff and the water—a perfect place to blow up, to cover with prepared fire. Even Lord Byron might have noted that. Just by the road, and partly in the lake, stood the Castle of Chillon, where for five centuries every kind of firearm known to man had been set to stop anything that moved. Opposite the castle was fake stonework, concealing the artillery behind it.

The highway soon became dual, and, approaching Saint-Maurice, had a divider made of cables, light-alloy posts, and wire mesh. Massy remarked that the posts were removable, from sleeves embedded in the concrete, and in a matter of minutes a few kilometres of divider could be carried to the side of the road. This is practiced at least once a year. From concealed bunkers, jets appear, roar up the highway, pass under bridges, rise into the sky.

At Saint-Maurice—epicenter of the western fortress, protector of the Valais, bastion of the Upper Rhone—the topography tightens, mountains draw close on both sides of the river, and the patterns of preset artillery fire probably resemble tartan.

"Je suis papa," said Massy. He had neglected to mention to Fantony that he had become a parent since his last course in the army.

"Félicitations!" said Fantony.

"Un garçon!" said Massy.

Fantony clapped his hands, applauding the brilliant performance.

Around Saint-Maurice, the Rhone Valley was essentially without vines, because the river runs north there and the slopes do not face the sun. At Martigny, however, the river, the road, and the entire landscape made a ninety-degree turn to the east, and now the prodigious vineyards of Valais were spread up the south-facing slopes. Out there in front of us we saw very high mountains, too, and Massy thought the snow line looked uncomfortably low. "Ai," he said. "The snow is too close. Two or three times, we will sleep outside."

"Perhaps we will not have to go so high."

"There will be rain below. These boots are not good in rain. They pump water."

The valley floor was three kilometres wide and as

flat as the lake bed it became when the ice melted. Apples, pears, cherries, the flatland was covered with orchards. The mountains went up steeply, like the sides of Massy's glass. The glacier had not been uniformly successful in cutting off the mountains' spurs, and where they had resisted strongly the big valley now and again seemed to pinch itself closed. Falling rock, in great quantity, had formed obstacles, too. Deep gorges broke the sides. It was wiser to enter this valley in a white Lancia than in a red tank.

There were towers of isolate rock standing in the valley—two at Sion, one at Raron—each supporting a castle or a church. James Fenimore Cooper preferred these rock eminences to the Acropolis: "The Acropolis does not overhang Athens in a more kingly style, than these rocks frown upon the humbler town of Sion, nor do I believe that the architecture of the former, however pure and classical, is half as picturesque." Cooper, travelling through here a hundred and fifty years ago, was even less attracted to the mountains than the shivering Massy. Cooper noted that the rock was "stern" and "naked," and that the mountains were "streaked with sterility."

Massy was in less than a hurry to report for active duty. His way of going into the army was to stop off at vineyards and call on friends—classmates, in effect, from Montagibert, the federal school for oenologists and viticulteurs. He stopped and toured a cave or two. He toured the Domaine du Mont d'Or, near Sion. In an atmosphere dreamy with the nose-tingling smell of fermentation, he looked at inflatable rubber presses and browsed over the labels in the company's Vinothèque. A sign above the bottles pleaded: "NE NOUS TOUCHEZ PAS! NOUS DORMONS!"

More wine comes out of Sion than any other place in the country, he remarked as we drove on up the road. Now the terraces on the valleyside reminded me of the football stadium at the University of Texas, where the side that holds the home crowd rises tier upon tier until people are seated in the sky. Switzerland produces about a hundred million litres a year, and consumes virtually all of it. Moreover, Switzerland imports two-thirds of what it drinks. Switzerland imports more Beaujolais than is imported by the United States. Dôle is the predominant red wine of the Valais, and the white is called Fendant. In my opinion, Fendant is guzzling-good wine. To compare it with his own, Massy extended himself to the limits of his generosity, saying, "Fendant will have less character, and be heavier, so you can drink one or two bottles, but maybe not more." Massy worked a season in the Napa Valley, attempting to expand his knowledge. Among the things he learned was that if you put wood chips in wine it will taste of oak.

At Turtmann, we passed a long airstrip, and five twin-boom jet Venoms happened to be emerging like lobsters from holes in the lateral rock. As jet fighters go, Venoms are something less than state of the art. They are used for instruction. "Would you believe it?" said Massy. "Those planes are partly made of wood."

The traffic—military trucks, cars, and to some extent the Venoms, too—was being delayed by a woman leading a herd of cows. She was riding a motorcycle and wearing a steel helmet.

The journey was almost over, the car approaching Brig. I mentioned to Massy that I had been told that Swiss militiamen could scarcely wait to get back into the army—that they looked forward to it from one year to the next. "Not everyone thinks alike," he said. "I do it because I have to, and because I think I can help a little bit—also to be equal with the others who do it." He went on to say that the "obsession" of most soldiers during basic training was not to be chosen to become a corporal and therefore possibly an officer. "It's O.K. for people in bureaus, but if you have your own proper business it's not. To be a captain is to spend almost two months of your year each year." He repeated that he was busy at home, the clouds looked unfriendly, and he could do without the cold mountain air. The clouds had spread out to reveal even higher peaks, like long gray razors scraping lather. "It is cold here," he complained. "Oh! It is cold." We had come into the outskirts of the small, medieval city where the Simplon Tunnel goes into the rock. Brig: where the Furka-Oberalp intersects the national railroad, where the highway ascends toward Italy, where a large part of the Fifth Regiment had been told to arrive at noon. At eleven-fifty-five, Massy drew into a parking slot at the railway station. Far up the platforms, all over the streets, everywhere we looked were soldiers. They filled up the station house, the Second Class Buffet, the booths in the postal telephone. We got out of the car. Massy buttoned his tunic. He cinched the leather belt around his waist. "Voilà," he said. "We're in the army now."

It seems likely that the two most widely circulated remarks ever made about Switzerland's military prowess were made by Napoleon Bonaparte and Orson Welles.

Welles said, "In Italy for thirty years under the Borgias, they had warfare, terror, murder, bloodshed—but they produced Michelangelo, Leonardo da Vinci, and the Renaissance. In Switzerland, they have brotherly love, five hundred years of democracy and peace, and what did that produce? The cuckoo clock."

Napoleon said, "The best troops—those in whom you can have the most confidence—are the Swiss."

Welles spoke his lines in "The Third Man," a motion picture that deservedly attracted an extensive worldwide audience. The screenplay was written by Graham Greene, who later published the preliminary treatment in book form, but Greene was not the author of the lines about the Borgias and Switzerland. They were interpolated by the ingenious Welles, who may have chosen to suppress in his memory the fact that when Italy was enjoying the Borgias, Switzerland was enjoying a reputation as—to quote Douglas Miller's "The Swiss at War"—"the most powerful and feared military force in Europe." Switzerland was about as neutral in those days as had been Mongolia under Genghis Khan. Not only were the Swiss ready to fight. They fought. They had a militia system that could mobilize fifty-four thousand soldiers. They knew enough warfare and bloodshed to sicken a Borgia. They were so chillingly belligerent that even if they were destroyed in battle they had been known in the same moment to win a war. One afternoon in mid-Renaissance, a few hundred Swiss who were outnumbered fifteen to one elected not to run away but to wade across a river and break into the center of the opposition, where all of them died, but not before they had slaughtered three thousand of their French enemies. The French Army was so unnerved that it struck its tents and fled.

It was the Swiss who unhorsed the mounted knight, and in a sense their confederation—their Everlasting League—was formed with that in mind. The peasants of the forest cantons made their pact of mutual defense because they wished not to be the vassals of alien equestrian lords. They waited twenty-four years for the first big test of their ability to resist—ample time to be prepared, to rehearse what they would do. Then, in 1315, two thousand Austrian knights appeared, leading a considerable army, and fatally attempted to make use of Morgarten pass. The knights were aristocrats, accustomed to tournament warfare and not to peasants attacking them from higher ground. The peasants came down on them with tree trunks, halberds, axes, and plummeting rock. The pass was blocked. The horses and riders became compressed and hopelessly jammed. The peasants rushed among them and hacked them down. Few knights survived. ("In the mountains, mechanization doesn't help you any. You are almost lost with armored cars.")

Also in the Renaissance, Swiss soldiers began sewing white crosses on their doublets, so they would recognize one another in the confusion of infantry battle. When mounted knights attacked them in open country, the Swiss formed squares—ten thousand soldiers in a square, bristling with twenty-one-foot pikes: the Porcupine Principle. In the course of time, they developed some interesting equipment. They developed the Lucerne hammer, fundamentally a poleaxe with a brass fist on its head and spikes protruding between the fingers. They developed the Morgenstern, an eight-foot cudgel with a sixteen-spike pineapple head. And they developed the Swiss Army knife.

Its precursor was a simple fifteenth-century dagger that every warrior carried. Over a hundred years, it acquired so many additions and complications that only officers and rich citizens could afford it, and it fell into disuse. It was an infantry weapon, but in its advanced stages it acquired built-in forks and other utensils. Competition waxed in the decorating of sheaths with scroll ornaments in gold and silver, and expensive foreign artists—such as the Hans Holbeins—were employed to do the work. The knife every soldier is issued today is jacketed with quilted gray aluminum, has one blade, a can opener, a bottle opener, a hole punch, two screw-drivers, and no corkscrew. On one side is a small red shield bearing the white cross. The knife is made identically by two companies—Victorinox and Wenger—that also make the red knives that in commercial display cases are all stuck apart like swastikas and include fish disgorgers, ski-wax scrapers, international wrenches, magnifying glasses, tweezers, toothpicks, scissors, and saws. The gray army knife resembles the simpler of the commercial offerings, minus the red plastic. Officers included, everyone in the Swiss Army carries a Swiss Army knife. Once, at the end of a long session in driving snow with machine guns firing and grenades exploding—up on the high ground where such practice can be conducted with live ammunition—I walked down with the Fifth Regiment's Colonel Marc-Henri Chaudet, and when he reached the roadhead he discovered that his automobile would not start. It was a gray Mercedes-Benz, and—with its hood up—its engine looked even grayer, there in the wind and stinging snow, many miles from the nearest garage and almost as many from the nearest warm room. After six hours of storm weather and steep inclines, the Colonel might have been forgiven if he had displayed exasperation. This, after all, was Switzerland, where everything works; Switzerland, where trains run like clocks, and clocks run like watches, and watches are synchronous with the pulse of the universe; Switzerland, where electric eyes watch underground parking spaces and turn on green lights when they are free; Switzerland, where electric eyes watch urinals and flush not only the one under address but the one next to it as well; Switzerland, where switches in mattresses cause rooms to go dark as people get into bed; and now, in Switzerland, the Colonel was inconvenienced by this weather-whipped, tuned-down, one-jewel German car, which wheezed but would not cough. Colonel Chaudet—a Vevey lawyer—gave it a cool glance, sighting along his nose. Tall, slim, handsome—his trousers taut and neatly creased and disappearing inside his boots like a downhill skier's—the Colonel had a certain downplay in the corners of his mouth, suggesting, among other things, detached amusement. Besides, he had complete confidence in his soldiers and their equipment. Observing the difficulty, a corporal stepped forward, removed from a pocket his Swiss Army knife, used a fingernail to expose the can opener, and leaned into the Mercedes. Within ten minutes, the engine was running.

The Swiss infantry, six hundred years ago, knew not only how to form a square but also how to break through almost anything. At Sempach—a name of resonance in Switzerland—a soldier named Arnold Winkelried gathered to his body the pike points of many foemen, thus opening on either side of him holes in the Austrian line, through which the Swiss backfield poured, swinging six-foot halberds, while Winkelried died. For each Swiss who died at Sempach, nine Austrians died as well, many of them dismounted knights. Machiavelli called the Swiss "the new Romans." In the Quattrocento, exactly three hundred years before the United States declared its independence, the Swiss won a great victory at a small town called Morat, defeating Burgundian invaders who were threatening the city of Fribourg. Among the Swiss ordnance were mortars that shot chunks of limestone and granite. Four hundred and ten Swiss died at Morat—and twelve thousand Burgundians. A durable legend sprang from this battle. To wit: a Swiss courier-soldier, carrying a linden branch, ran with the glorious news to Fribourg; all but breathless, he at last approached the ramparts and the towers of the town, and passed through the main gate and into the central square, where anxious Fribourgeois had formed a human circle—magistrates, priests, women on their knees—in the center of which the courier gathered his last three breaths, shouted "Victoire! Victoire! Victoire!" and fell dead, as later recorded, "la face contre terre." It has been suggested that this story is not without companionship in a genre. However that may be, there is an old sick linden in Fribourg that is thought to have grown from the branch the runner carried. Each year, in October, a footrace is run from Morat to Fribourg, and it now attracts about a hundred thousand spectators and eleven thousand runners. The race has been held for fifty years, with runners sometimes preparing for the ordeal by stretching their minds as well as their muscles—chanting in the streets, "Morat! Morat! Morat!" It doesn't matter that the distance is four-tenths of a marathon.

Swiss neutrality began in 1515, when the Swiss were thoroughly beaten by a French Army under François I at Marignano, in what is now Italy. "I have conquered those whom only Caesar managed to conquer before me," said the French king, and his words were struck in coin. The confederated cantons, by then thirteen, decided to fight thereafter only as mercenaries in other people's wars. They were a small nation, rustic, poor—nothing at all like the service-industry and manufacturing society we know today—and to embellish their economy they leased their incomparable soldiers. The cantons have always been importantly autonomous, and never more so than in the sixteenth century, when the political bond between Catholics and Protestants was under so much strain. It is unlikely that during the heaviest reverberations of the Reformation a co-operating army could have been assembled from the Protestant and Catholic cantons, and so, regardless of Marignano, neutrality was now less a matter of policy than a de-facto condition of Swiss life. The militia was then, as it has generally remained, cantonal in character. The cantons did the selling of soldiers. The French bought heavily for three hundred years—now twelve thousand Swiss, now seventy thousand Swiss, now a hundred and sixty-three thousand Swiss, depending on the intensity of the problems of France. For all that time, the Compagnie des Cent-Suisses were the personal bodyguards of the French kings. Scarcely had the Swiss soldiers appeared in the French court when the Pope decided that he wanted some, too; and the Pope, of course, still has them, ninety in all—the only vestige of the Swiss mercenaries.

Switzerland is so conscious—not to say proud—of the service of its mercenaries in foreign armies that a château outside Geneva has been refurbished as a Musée des Suisses à l'Étranger. The most eminent mercenary of all was Colonel Louis Pfyffer, Roi des Suisses, who became a Swiss hero by serving four French kings. Jérôme d'Erlach, of Bern, became a Swiss hero as an Austrian field marshal. François Lefort, of Geneva, became a Swiss hero as a Russian general under Peter the

Great, as Viceroy of the Grand Duchy of Novgorod, as President of all the Councils of Russia, and as the creator and Grand Admiral of the Russian Navy. Swiss mercenaries fought for the Scandinavian kingdoms, the Holy Roman Empire, the Netherlands, Prussia, Poland, Lorraine, Saxony, Savoy, Spain. In various battles, they fought on both sides. They served the Doge of Genoa, the King of Naples, the Elector of Brandenburg. For a large unnegotiable discount, they served Napoleon. Later, they became one of the perennially toughest components of the French Foreign Legion. In the Château de Penthes—the Musée des Suisses à l'Étranger—hangs a British Union Jack with a prominently inset Swiss white cross.

Contracts always specified that if Switzerland was attacked the soldiers would go back to Switzerland. All such contracts have been illegal for something over a hundred years. Meanwhile, by 1830 or so, in places like Bière, the militias of the various cantons were getting together to march, to exercise, to perform military legerdemain before people with parasols and uncorked wine, men in top hats chatting with soldiers in uniform attending the beginning of the federal army. Upward of a hundred thousand people will turn out today to watch the army parade and perform. A retired soldier will visit his unit's refresher course like an old college football player returning to watch a practice. Quite voluntarily, several thousand civilian soldiers annually collect for a thirty-kilometre footrace in which they carry packs and rifles. Beneath the long neutrality, there lies what the Swiss describe as "an aptitude for war." It appears to be an appetite as well—sublimated and under close control.

La Place de la Concorde Suisse

The Landesmuseum in Zurich is the Louvre of the toy soldier. In glass cases there, toy soldiers by the ten thousand engage in replica battles. There are eight military museums in La Suisse Romande alone. In Morges, there are displays not only of Swiss military exploits but also of Aztec sacrifices, the Siege of Alesia (52 b.c.), and the Battle of Zama, with elephants. In the rooms the women come and go talking of Saint-Lô.

The money brought home by mercenary soldiers started Switzerland's banks. In the foyer of the Federal Assembly, in Bern, stand sculptures of four Swiss soldiers—one armed with a halberd, one with a pike, and two with broadswords. Through heavy bronze doors is the Bundesplatz, surrounded on three sides exclusively by contiguous banks, and on the fourth by the national capitol. To this day, what gives Swiss banks their special distinction is not their corporate inventiveness, which is on the level of the Marble Savings Bank, of Rutland, Vermont, but their fortresslike security, which is emphasized by the Swiss Army. More often than not, a high-ranking officer in a Swiss bank will also be a high-ranking officer in the army. The foremost banks—the Three Sisters of Swiss banking—are the Schweizerischer Bankverein, the Schweizerische Bankgesellschaft, and the Schweizerische Kreditanstalt, better known around the world as Crédit

Suisse. The general manager of the Bankverein is Major Walter Frehner. The president of the Bankgesellschaft is Colonel Niklaus Senn. The chief executive officer of Crédit Suisse is Colonel Robert Jeker. In contrast to all other countries, there is in Switzerland a positive correlation between military rank and economic leadership generally. Colonel Fritz Gerber is the chairman of the board of Hoffmann–La Roche. Major Louis von Planta is the chairman of the board of Ciba-Geigy. Chemical companies, insurance companies, construction companies are under the command of majors, colonels, brigadiers.

There is nothing honorific about the military service of these men. They spend one day out of ten in the army. They command battalions, regiments, brigades. The army, in addition to all its other functions, has long been considered a first-rate school of business management. A major commands a battalion of eight hundred. It seems absolutely logical to the Swiss that if a man can lead eight hundred people in military service he can lead a department of that size in civilian life. The special training required for a position on the general staff is looked upon as the equivalent of two years at the Harvard Business School. The Bankgesellschaft, like the army, has a series of special schools through which its officers rise in rank: an assistant-vice-president school, a vice-president school, a first-vice-president school. The bankers receive orders telling them where to report to school. If you ask a Swiss banker whether his army service has affected his position in the bank, he will usually say something like "Oh, indeed, yes. Now I have this special staff job because of my position in the army." Of course, some banks (and manufacturing and service companies) are more military-minded than others. On the French side of the country, being a "military head" can actually be a disadvantage. There are at least two bank presidents who march with the rank and file. (Switzerland has more than five hundred banking institutions.) An army captain has told me that he once leaped to his feet because the soldier serving him food was an executive vice-president of the company he worked for in Basel. To be high in business and low in the army is less unusual than the reverse; it is rare, perhaps even difficult, for someone to remain low in business while attaining high status in the army. Some corporations actually insist that their employees pursue the highest achievable military rank. When an important business promotion is reported in the press, the notice might say, typically, "He is thirty-seven years old, is married, has three children, lives in Rapperswil, and is a major in the mountain infantry."

During Robert Jeker's parallel rise from soldier to colonel and from trainee to chief executive officer and president of the executive board of Crédit Suisse, he served fifteen hundred days in the army—an average of fifty days a year for thirty years. To Crédit Suisse, this was something more than a patriotic donation of time; it was also a gain for the bank. "The skills you get in one place help you in the other place," Jeker explained to me one day in his office in Zurich. "In the army, we meet people from every level of the community. We come to understand other professions, other companies, other parts of the country. We make business contacts. It helps that we know these people from the army. We are with them twenty-four hours a day.

We know them better than in business life." He paused, and added, "If this bank is choosing a new manager, military record is not one of the major points, but it is never a disadvantage. It will never be negative that someone has to be away from the bank for military service."

Jeker worked in the United States for two and a half years and regularly went home to serve as a second lieutenant. He worked in Paris, Florence, and Buenos Aires, and yet was enabled to spend enough time in Switzerland to become not only a colonel but also a member of the general staff—promotions that demand a great deal of extra time. "It's usual that you are a member of the army," he said. "If not, a part of your life is missing. When we sit together in private life, we often talk about the army. Your conscience can accept it more thoroughly when you know you will attack no one." A tall straightforward man with a guileless smile, Jeker did not advertise in his manner either his high military station or his civilian status as a supergnome. Taking note that he had spent thirty-five days in the army last year and at the same time had been preparing to assume command of one of the most powerful banks in the world, I asked him what he did for a vacation. Where on earth could he go—where had he most recently been—to get away on his own from both the bank and the army?

"Alaska," he said.

Military service is subsidized by industry in various ways. A soldier in a refresher course gets four Swiss francs a day—not enough to pay for an evening's beer. All the while, however, he is being paid as usual by his civilian company, and the government's reimbursement to the company is only seventy per cent—and, of course, the lost work is irrecoverable. An officer uses company telephones to call all over Switzerland on matters having to do with his military unit. He uses the company Xerox, the company computer, his own and his secretary's time—to an extent that varies in direct proportion to the military-mindedness of the supreme executive. If the supreme executive is a Militärkopf, anything goes and the bill will be paid. If a general-staff officer happens to work for Ciba-Geigy in Summit, New Jersey, Ciba-Geigy will pay his way home to serve.

The higher a man rises in the army, the more of his time—by a very large factor—his company gives, for army time in no way invades vacation time. Everyone in the army has his "Little Book of Service," recording, like a pilot's flying time, his total number of service days, and including bare details of the experience—a military scrapbook in efficient form and of such metaphorical reach in Switzerland that Max Frisch has written a book using its title: "Dienstbüchlein." The basic-training period for everyone is seventeen weeks. During basic training, a number of soldiers are invited to become corporals—an advance that requires a hundred and forty-five extra days. This is what Massy did his best to avoid, and his best was good enough. In thirty years of faithful service, Massy as a plain soldier will record in his "Dienstbüchlein" a grand total approximating three hundred and sixty-five days. Colonel Rainer von Falkenstein—just to choose someone for contrast—has already served thirteen hundred days, is only lightly pushing fifty, and will have recorded nearly two thousand days when he retires. Even before he earned his Ph.D. in chemistry, he had served six hundred and fifty days as a machine gunner—a family tradition. The other six hundred and fifty days—as an army specialist in chemical and nuclear weapons—have come out of his employment at the Sandoz pharmaceutical company. It is all in his "Little Book of Service."

Any rise in rank costs many extra days. Serving them is known as "paying your grade." Corporals with a certain something about them are invited to become lieutenants, and for that they pay two hundred and thirty-six days. After leading a section for a number of three-week refresher courses, a lieutenant may be invited to become a captain, and the price for that is a hundred and sixty-five days—while Massy racks wine. As an oenologist, he has formed the opinion that the wine will not become memorable as a result of his being a major, but it could become insipid. Not everyone who is self-employed takes the same short view. Lawyers find the army an excellent milieu for the development of practice. Salesmen in uniform go right on selling. School-teachers, who acquire an essentially fixed status at the outset of their careers, tend to seek in the army the rewards and reassurance of promotion.

Certain captains—described as "a crème-de-la-crème élite"—are invited to become candidates for the general staff, which, as in any army, makes plans, forms strategy, and integrates operations. At least five separate courses must be passed to achieve the distinction, and so much additional service that the days are difficult to count. Doctors, lawyers drop aside; they haven't the time. Corporations underwrite the general staff. The exact number of general-staff officers is classified but is something like two thousand. If a corporation has in its hierarchy fifty military officers, possibly two will be on the general staff. There is, of course, no published list. One cannot look these people up. But—Jeker, Heusser, Hupfauf, Bührle—being on the general staff is not a personal secret. A man would list it on his résumé. It is said that a corporation expects fifty per cent more of a member of the general staff, even if he is away eight weeks a year. To perform an exercise all night in rain and then get ready for sleep only to be called out again for some hours and then denied sleep again in order to confront a new situation—and so on for fifty-six consecutive hours—is to undergo training for the general staff. "It was the most stressful time of my life. I would do it again. You are under pressure. You have to make decisions. You are alone. You have to learn. It is good executive training. It is more rigorous than Harvard."

Something under half the general staff are full-time army officers, whose principal function is teaching, in basic-training schools and refresher courses. To learn what they are to teach, some of them are sent to the Swiss Federal Institute of Technology, in Zurich, and they also go abroad. They study at the German general-staff college, in Hamburg. They study at the École Supérieure de Guerre, in Paris, and the Royal College of Defence Studies, in London. They can be found regularly in United States Army schools at Fort Benning, Fort Leavenworth, and Fort Knox. Thoroughgoing professionals, they can be numbered in the low hundreds. In the Swiss Army as a whole, there are fifty thousand officers who are neither professionals nor members of the general staff, and what is most remarkable about them is—businessmen, bankers—how professional they appear coming out from behind their desks. It is impossible to say that the face becomes the mask, or the mask becomes the face, because the colonel and the barrister, the banker and the captain, the major and the businessman are one. In their uniforms, there might be a faint whiff of mothballs, but not in their military presence. Spread through the country with their troops, they suggest such establishment of command that they seem to be alumni of a West Point, of which Switzerland has no counterpart more exact than its banks.

Observed in their cadres, wearing their gold stripes and tailored green, as, say, they dine together in regimental headquarters at the Hotel Rhone, in Salgesch, they are—from Day One of a repetition course—very evidently cohesive, hierarchical, serious, and believably military, no matter where they may have been the day before. There is an atmosphere of shared experience. Companionable, familiar, they seem to belong together, and, from nuance to nuance, to speak their common language uncommonly in common. As one captain has delicately phrased it for me, "we don't want to have an upper-class officers' corps, but on the other hand it is not easy for a plumber or a mason to be with the officers." They are somewhat St. Paul's. That is, they are essentially old school, and in fundament ecclesiastic. Chaplains pray with them in the morning and bring them benediction at night. They break their croissants at six-thirty sharp. Beforehand, the young chaplain of the day may have brought greetings from his uncle, a retired colonel, and then used phrases like "No problem" while comparing life to a crossword puzzle wherein the vertical is love of God, the horizontal is love of man, and the two together form the cross. Seated at a long table and flanking Colonel Chaudet, they appear to be convened for the Last Breakfast. More than half of them have—or are working on—advanced degrees. Colonel Chaudet is said to be working on a possible candidacy for a place on the Federal Council, whose seven ministers are collectively the supreme national executive. His father, Paul Chaudet, was Minister of Defense some time ago, and twice took his turn as President of Switzerland. The Colonel is cool, a little shy, somewhat distant. Often, one hears said of him, "C'est le fils de son père." In their bright, evening moods, the officers sometimes call to mind stage scenes of old Heidelberg, as if the river nearby were, for the moment, the Neckar instead of the Rhone. Not a great deal of time has gone by since the days of the student fighting societies, which were as prevalent in Switzerland as in Germany—the Alt Helvetia Society, the Tigurinia Society, the Jurassia and Germania Societies—wherein the young future officers in the universities went at each other with one-metre swords. It was a tradition. They did not fight to "win," they fought to develop fearlessness and other forms of courage.

When I learned that Dr. Max Taeschler, a friend of mine in Basel, had belonged in his youth to such a society, I asked him, "Did you cut each other?"

He said, "Only in the head."

In Salgesch, over raclette and Fendant, I remarked one evening to the captain on my right that the atmosphere among the assembled officers suggested an English or American gentlemen's club. "That is an excellent definition of the army," he said. "That is it—exactly."

The major on my left commented frankly that he had put a great deal of effort into his military career, in part for patriotism and in part for the rank, because of its advantage in the civilian world.

The captain concluded, "If you are going to have a close tie between the citizenry and the army, you have to have an effect on the society, including the closing of some doors to non-army people. That, of course, is criticized."

In days largely gone by, to be a sergeant was more important in a village than to be a priest or the mayor. To become an officer was—in one's family—a matter of triumph or tradition. Not to be accepted for military service was a family shame. These durable criteria have diminished but have not disappeared. To be turned down by the army is a financial liability if not a complete shame. Doors close in the commercial world.

There are those also who do not accept service—two or three hundred young men each year who for religious and conscientious reasons refuse to serve—and doors are closed to them in the most emphatic way: they are tried in court and sent to jail. Sentences range from four to six months. Swiss Mennonites who refused to carry arms emigrated long ago to places like Iowa and Pennsylvania. Only on the ground of mental or physical unfitness can a Swiss male citizen be legally excused from the army, unless he happens to be a policeman or hold some other deferment job. The list is short. In 1977, a hundred thousand Swiss signed a petition that put on the ballot an initiative calling for alternative ways to do national service—hospital work or whatever. Eight to five, the people voted it down. The Federal Council has recently decreed that a soldier with his colonel's permission may serve without a gun. There is now a petition in circulation that calls for an initiative to abolish the army altogether. An initiative to abolish chocolate would stand an equal chance.

There are remarkably few graffiti in Switzerland. The most distinguished is Lord Byron's name, by his own hand, in the dungeon that held the prisoner of Chillon. The most intense are the terse initials that equate the Helvetian Confederation with the Third Reich: "CH = SS." A surprising number are in English: "STONED AGAIN," "KILL THE PIGS NOW," "THE SHIP'S A-GOIN' DOWN." Most of all, one sees the circled "A" of the anarchist youth movement that has ruffled the complacency of the republic with protest in recent years but seems for the moment to have subsided, to have acquired a complacency of its own. The circled "A"s increase in number with proximity to Zurich, proximity to Basel, proximity to Geneva. Generally speaking, the acceptance and esteem that the army enjoys among contemporary youth in Switzerland are in direct proportion to distance from cities.

"Can we count on the young generation? Yes. Yes. Yes. Be careful on this question. As commander of a regiment, I have found that young people in the seventeen weeks' basic training might cause trouble for one or two weeks only. After that, their psychological problems are negligible, and more or less don't exist."

"Basel, Geneva, and Zurich are not representative of Switzerland. There are critical, negative youngsters in cities. Youngsters are completely different in the Mittelland farm country and certainly in the mountains. If there are troubles, they are in the big towns."

"The army is an educational matter in Switzerland —not only a question of defense. Every Swiss age twenty needs to be shouted at a little and to have a good time with friends. He becomes a citizen who has a gun at home."

Young athletes, whose years of maximum ability are so elusively brief, have been known to appear at the army health examination with their bloodstreams full of alcohol, so their hearts would flutter like caged birds. Some are adept at simulating deafness in one ear. Not many are rejected outright. La Commission de Recrutement assigns them instead to the Service Complémentaire, to do a hundred days' duty over ten years— clerklike, without weapons. One Swiss athlete who quite undeceptively ended up in the Service Complémentaire was Jean-François Pahud, a first-rank distance runner twenty years ago. He was known throughout the nation as Le Long Pahud—a reference to his remarkable physique. Towering above the doctor in the examination room, Pahud, who could run five kilometres in fourteen and a half minutes, was told that he was unfit for the army because his chest was too small. To qualify for the Swiss Army, a man's chest circumference had to be half his height, and Pahud's was far from it. He was told to do certain exercises and return in a year. A year later, age twenty, Pahud returned. His chest had become even smaller. "Like all Swiss youth, I saw the army as a test of manhood," he recalls. "I hoped to be an officer. Only later did other athletes point out to me how lucky I was."

In the Service Complémentaire, he found the other athletes: the Swiss record holder in the shot put, the European record holder at two hundred metres.

Albert Einstein, who became a Swiss citizen at the age of twenty-one, was also rejected by the regular army. He had varicose veins and flat feet, and was assigned, like Le Long Pahud, to the Service Complémentaire.

Women may join the Service Complémentaire. For them, it is voluntary, but once they sign up they serve for fifteen years. They drive vehicles. They operate telephone and radio systems. They cook. They tend homing pigeons. I have heard all that referred to as "housewife work." Switzerland in 1981 passed a law assuring equality of rights to women and men—an equivalent of the Equal Rights Amendment, and a large step for a nation that only ten years before gave women the right to vote in national elections. In Appenzell, women still cannot vote in cantonal elections. There are no women on the general staff.

Jean-François Pahud is now the curator of the Olympic Museum, in Lausanne. A tall man with a great wash of silver-edged black hair, a prominent nose, a large black mustache, he remains more slender than a finishing nail. In the event of a national emergency, he says, every athlete would be on hand to do something about it.

Does he feel there is a need for an army in Switzerland?

He replies, "C'est clair."

With other parts of the battalion, Massy and the Section de Renseignements reported at noon to the garage in Brig where the bureaucracy of the Poste-Téléphone-Télégraphe regionally services its numerous buses, all of which were out on the road. The room was as big as an armory. The soldiers lined up to be issued sleeping bags, mountain jackets, rain capes, gaiters, Finnish hats, and surgical bandages. Thus their refresher course began, and they sat on their packs and waited. Lieutenant Wyssa waited. Captain Dessemontet. Massy, at the center of a cluster of soldiers, removed from his pack a bottle of wine. Massy's pack looked like a launcher of ground-to-air missiles. He began his refresher course with his tire-bouchon, raising the cork. He ran it past his nose, and unbuttoned his breast pocket, reaching for his little glass. "The purpose of the Section de Renseignements is to eliminate uncertainty," he said, addressing no one in particular, expecting nothing in return—erupting with mock instructions and aping the tone of an officer, as he often does, apparently to enjoy the sound as it raps the air. Following his ritual, he filled the glass, wished good health to the soldiers around him, and drank. Then he filled it again, for Pascal Layaz, twenty-two years old, a graphic artist from Vevey, who wears a gold ring in one ear; for Pierre Pillard, twenty-seven years old, a redheaded, red-bearded fitter of false teeth, who works in Yverdon; for Christian Tanniger, Michel Frei, Bernard Parisod, housepainters, of Lausanne, Vevey, Montreux; for Jean-Bruno Wettstein, of Nyon. Reporting to Brig, in Valais, they were all from the Canton de Vaud. Regiments still belong to the cantons, which have not transferred to the federal government nearly as much right or power as have the states of the United States. A person who earns, say, twenty thousand francs a year in the Canton de Vaud owes taxes of less than a hundred francs to the confederation and eighteen hundred to the canton. A person who earns a hundred thousand francs pays six thousand to the confederation and twenty-three thousand to the canton. If a canton needs troops, it can take two battalions from any of its regiments without requesting them of the confederation. In Lausanne, the capital of Vaud, a green bronze statue dominates the plaza between the Château Saint-Maire and the house of the Grand Council. It is a likeness of Charles Veillon (1809–69), described on the plinth as "Colonel of the Army of Vaud."

In the bus garage, the proud soldiers seemed pleased to be seeing one another—as who would not be, through the bottom of Massy's glass? There was more to being

La Place de la Concorde Suisse

in the army than being in the army: they were back together. Sometimes in the civilian year, they have their small reunions. As an adjutant began shouting orders, each order was mimicked by someone obscure in the crowd. Massy smiled and poured the wine. Generally speaking, it can be said that discipline is nearly perfect in the Swiss Army, and that discipline is perhaps a little less than perfect if the soldiers are thinking in French, and, finally, that within any French-speaking battalion perfection tends to dilapidate in the Section de Renseignements. According to majors and manuals, Renseignements is an activity that calls for a special style of mind, constantly seeking intelligence and finding it even if it is not there, for in peacetime exercises what is required above all else is imagination. The effect of the Section de Renseignements is, in one major's words, "to make it live." The patrols of Renseignements walk in the unoccupied territory between the battalion and the enemy. They circle high behind enemy lines. Since the mountains are real and the enemy is not, there tends to be a certain diminution of energy during a refresher course—particularly on the part of those who go out on patrol, in contrast to those who stay in the command post and think up things for the patrols to do. Essentially, the people in the command posts are editors, trying to make sense of the information presented by the patrols, and by and large the patrols are collections of miscellaneous freelancing loners, who lack enthusiasm for the military enterprise, have various levels of antipathy to figures of authority, and, in a phrase employed by themselves and their officers alike, are "the black sheep of the army."

Of the five companies in each battalion, it is the Headquarters Company that includes the Section de Renseignements. Soldiers in the Section de Renseignements are drawn from each of the four other companies. More often than not, the captains choose from their companies soldiers they want to get rid of.

"Massy, did they want to get rid of you?"

"But yes."

"But why?"

"I have spent many days in le trou."

Le trou—known formally as the local d'arrêts and the arrestlokal—is where soldiers are locked up after they come in late at night, for example, or fail to clean their rifles, or drink themselves to paralysis, or go to sleep on watch, or shoot at téléphérique cables and high-tension wires. It is where many people thought a number of soldiers should have been put after they shot at center-fold photographs from *Playboy*. A captain can give three days in le trou, a major ten, a colonel fifteen. The soldier is locked up with a Bible.

"He has a window now."

"Because of the human rights."

When bullets hit high-tension wires, the wires flash with flame. When the soldiers used *Playboy* pictures as assault-rifle targets, the story was reported in newspapers and feminists burst into flame. The army said the fusiliers had shown bad taste. Various amici curiae asked why the women had let themselves be photographed in the first place—a question lacking an answer that would satisfy a Swiss.

Massy yanked at a pétard on a lieutenant's chest and got ten days in le trou. There was more to the story, of course, than just that. A pétard is a small imitation grenade—basically a firecracker. Like a grenade, it has a fuse, and it explodes six and a half seconds after the fuse is activated. The playful Massy intended to remove the pétard, fuse and all, from the lieutenant's chest, but the lieutenant slapped at Massy's hand and Massy succeeded only in activating the fuse. Six, five, four . . . There were fifty pétards on the lieutenant's chest. After the first one exploded, others sequentially exploded, too. The lieutenant became a walking sparkler. As Massy describes him, "he was running around like Donald Duck." Attempting to stop the chain reaction, the lieutenant took off his steel helmet and clasped it to his chest. There was great thunder and a burst of lightning as all the remaining pétards exploded together. Massy was paler than a white grape. He thought the lieutenant was "finished." The lieutenant, as it happened, was completely uninjured, needed only a new uniform—and it was Massy who, for the nonce, was finished.

Pillard—the denture technician—reacted against all authority throughout his seventeen weeks of basic training and thereafter found a home in Renseignements. Later, at Trient, on the road to Chamonix, Pillard refused to obey a corporal who wanted him to do some extra work, and he spent ten days in le trou.

Jean-Bruno Wettstein, as a result of his first repetition course, was among the select who were invited to seek promotion. He went to a doctor instead. He said he had no desire to command anything and did not believe in the army. He said he could not accept the phenomenon of war, believing it to be "absurd and stupid." The doctor told him that if he was not careful he would be coded psycho in federal files and the label would hamper him for the rest of his life. The doctor wrote a letter that emphasized both Wettstein's sanity and the extreme difficulty he seemed to have in accepting authority. Wettstein was excused from the army for two years. He went to Gascony and worked with goats. "We were going to change the world," Wettstein said of himself and others. "But the world did not change, and we did." Eventually, when he rejoined the battalion, he was, in his words, "almost automatically put into Renseignements."

The soldiers were dressed now in their gaiters, their mountain jackets, their Finnish hats. Packs on their backs, rifles across their chests, they left the P.T.T. garage and walked half a mile through the quiet streets of Brig. They were on their way to La Prise du Drapeau, a ceremony in which the battalion would bring forth from storage its hallowed flag, to be carried into putative battle.

"It symbolizes our fighting spirit," someone remarked.

And Wettstein said, "Fighting spirit is very important in football games."

Wettstein, once a long-distance runner, continues to be in fine condition through his work in the alpages. With amiable brown eyes and a ready smile, he softens the bite of his words. Straight brown hair lightly touches his shoulders. He is the son of a radiologist, and he grew up in Geneva, a city that, in his words, is full of "bad Swiss." One year, as an exchange student, he went to Linn-Mar High School, in Marion, Iowa, where he won his "L-M" in track. "The Republic and Canton of Geneva has been in the confederation only since 1815," he said, explaining his remark about his home town. "It is an international city with no strong Swiss traditions." Genevans sometimes say that it is not necessary to be stupid to be a colonel but it helps.

Passing German street signs and German shop signs, the soldiers walked through town to hear a speech in French.

"Who will speak?"

"The major."

"What will he say?"

"He will say, 'The purpose of the army is to keep Switzerland free. The Russians are not very far away. Have a good three weeks. Dismissed.' "

The soldiers left their packs in a small meadow and formed ranks on a green beside a school. In various directions, there was little to see but light industry, a church steeple, small apartment buildings, sheep, cattle, and fruit trees—until you looked up. Everywhere above were Alps—gold, red, and green on the lower slopes, white beyond the timberline: Glishorn, Hübschhorn, Klenenhorn, the framing peaks of Simplon; Riederhorn, Hohstock, Sparrhorn, ascending the Bernese Oberland. Clouds were streaming up the mountainsides, running through the conifers like smoke. All five companies of the Eighth Battalion were assembled at parade rest and waiting. The Divisionnaire arrived, and the regimental colonel, Chaudet—the Divisionnaire in a white Mercedes, the Colonel in his gray one. Lesser officers lined up flanking Tschumy and Chaudet, including Captain François Rumpf, of the Bankverein; Major Peter Keller, of Hoffmann–La Roche; Colonel Louis Gilliéron, of La

Suisse Assurances; and Major Jean-Daniel Favre, of the Schweizerische Industrie Gesellschaft.

The five companies stood and silently waited. The Divisionnaire, the Colonel, and the lesser officers waited. The Alps waited. Time came and went forever while they waited for the band. It is a tradition among Swiss Army musicians that Swiss Army musicians are unique and special and deserve to be treated as such, in a class by themselves, above schedules and—like nothing else in Switzerland—beyond the clock.

Captain Rumpf whispered, "They are prima donnas."

Thirty minutes after the Divisionnaire had appeared, the band showed up, wearing old steel combat helmets of the sort that faced west across the Western Front. They puffed with effort on their tubas and bassoons, and—unlike the waiting soldiers—could in no sense be described as élite. They were middle-aged, for the most part, with beards of assorted lengths and paunches as prominent as drums. They appeared to have come out of an American Legion hall on the edge of River City. They might have been holding their thirty-fifth reunion. With emotion, elegance, stateliness, they played the national anthem.

The flag was carried forth, and Major Jacques-Henri Beausire stood in a jeep and addressed his battalion. "Officiers, sous-officiers, soldats . . ."

Major Beausire, an independent economic entrepreneur, is a former banker, whose brush-cut hair and firm heavy build more readily suggested an emeritus fullback.

"Ce matin, vous avez déjà accompli un des moments difficiles. . . ."

The speech was inconvenienced by a Toyota fork-lift in a marble yard next door.

". . . laisser les siens pour une période de trois semaines . . ."

The machine sporadically burped, and only fragments of the speech came through.

". . . quitter son activité professionelle malgré les soucis de la période économique que nous traversons. . . ."

Seven tons of rock fell off the fork.

"Je sais que vous aurez à cœur de démontrer que les gens de votre âge ne correspondent pas forcément à l'image de la minorité qui nous est abondamment rapportée et décrite par les moyens d'information. . . ."

As the soldiers left the ceremony, Wettstein parroted the Major, saying, " 'You are here now and have made a great sacrifice to leave your homes and jobs. You are representing the nation and not a discontented minority of youth. . . .' It is the same speech always," he said. "It is the same speech as in the States."

Massy said, "It is written by the same person."

When I have not been
out walking and collecting information with the Section
de Renseignements, I have been in the charge of Captain
Rumpf, whose "Little Book of Service" shows eleven
hundred days. The latter ones may have been trying for
him. It is possible that Rumpf would prefer to be crawling under machine-gun bullets. After I made application
to the government in Bern—and was softwared, dos-
siered, and cleared—I received letters informing me that
I would "serve" with units of the Tenth Mountain
Division and be under the general surveillance of Captain
François Rumpf. He is an adjutant of Divisionnaire
Tschumy, and has completed two or three months of
special training to become a major, which is not quite
enough; as a final requirement he has been given the task
of overseeing me. I alone stand between Rumpf and the
broad gold stripe of a major.

Rumpf is forty-one. He married Juliette Roussy, a

daughter of the Dean of the Cathedral of Lausanne, and has three young daughters. When I first met him, in Basel, he was wearing a Cardin blazer, a yellow V-necked cashmere pullover, a white-collared blue-and-white-striped shirt, and an English club tie. My own daughters would call him megaprep. With his apple cheeks and boyish manner, he did seem like a teacher at Uppingham or Kent, but he proved to be in charge of all private customers, worldwide, for the Schweizerischer Bankverein. He appreciatively acknowledges that he was given the job because of his rank in the army. The son of two doctors, he grew up in Vevey. His surname notwithstanding, he is resolutely Suisse romand—pure Vaudois and so much so that he regards Geneva as "absolutely not a Swiss town," and goes on to remark, "You will see a lot of Arabs there." In one of those moments of amazed recognition when someone exclaims "It's a small world!" Rumpf genteelly disagrees. "I say it is not a small world," says Rumpf. "I say the upper class is thin." He served the Bankverein for eight years in Monaco, and is now posted to Basel, from which he sends his children—Sophie, Joelle, Laetitia—daily into France to school. His ancestors lived in Basel, but he says the people of Basel today would never understand his Bentley (which he keeps in France). They might regard as rather odd his passion for distinguished cars.

The army has given him and me a sick Opel. We get around, seeing people and exercises. We go into the hanging valleys. Rumpf is an aesthetician. He likes sunsets, snow-covered couloirs, vines in fruit, and Switzerland. He points out the lovely, rock-enlofted church in Raron—where Rainer Maria Rilke is buried by the south-facing wall—and on the road to Simplon he ignores the hidden cannons. He tends to treat the army itself as if it were a military secret.

We went into the Val d'Anniviers. The dendritic valleys of Valais, branches of the Rhone system—Blinnental, Lötschental, Mattertal, Val de Bagnes, Val d'Hérens, Val d'Anniviers—are so competitively beautiful that (as with most awards) no one valley can reasonably be chosen above all others. Having said that, if I could go into only one I would without hesitation go into the Val d'Anniviers. Up out of the Rhone Valley we climbed the switchbacks from Sierre. We were discussing events that might occur in a time of national emergency, and I was asking Captain Rumpf how the army might respond if an enemy were to insist that Switzerland surrender or be showered with atomic bombs.

"We will absolutely never give up," he said. "Ninety-five per cent of Switzerland is sheltered, and we are on our way to a hundred per cent."

We were passing through the village of Niouc. Already, we were twelve hundred feet above the Rhone, and the mountainsides close around us went up six thousand more. Moving on along the keelson of the Val d'Anniviers, we could see ahead of us some of the high Pennines—Grand Cornier, Dent Blanche, Ober-Gabelhorn. "Do not bring a tank into this valley," Rumpf counselled me. "You would be blown to pieces."

The deeply cutting river was called La Navisence. Villages, spread in the sun on their alpages, were two thousand feet above the river. Other villages—Saint-Luc, Saint-Jean—were on lower ground, the chalets dark and plain. In Grimentz, there was a waterwheel and dark granaries standing on flat round stones, and notices on the walls: "AVIS DE TIR." The people are the first to know when bullets will be flying. About fifteen kilometres from the Rhone, we moved close among the buildings of a town called Mission, where Rumpf parked beside a public hall. It had been a school—one large room on an upper floor—and for the moment it was the brain center of the regiment's Seventh Battalion.

"I'll just look in a moment and see if anyone's here," said Rumpf.

Major Jean-Philippe Jaussi was there, and Captain Ernst Sturzenegger, finishing, with other officers, their midday meal. "Come and join us," said Jaussi. "There is plenty." The old schoolroom was touchingly spare— a heavy-plank unfinished floor, a long refectory table— with a spread of windows, mountain light, and absent paper snowflakes. The food, presented with a dated menu, was remarkably unspare—a flavorsome light potage, choux-rouge braisés, fresh saucisson and jambon fumé, pommes natures, Poire Belle-Hélène—and in the glassware was a vigorous Dôle of the Valais. Captain Sturzenegger—a youthful man with a quick-forming grin—said in the course of conversation that in his civilian job with Crédit Suisse he was in charge of all the bank's personnel outside Switzerland: the nation's modern mercenaries.

Rumpf said, "You see the influence of banking on the army."

And someone said, "Not to mention the influence of the army on banking."

I remarked that Ernst Sturzenegger was a name

roughly twice as German as François Rumpf, and I wondered how Sturzenegger had come to serve in a Suisse-
romand battalion.

Indeed, he was from Zurich, he said, and nothing
about him was French but his colleagues in the army.
In officer school, he had been told to translate something
into French and had done so with ease. He was also sent
out on a long walk, which he did not complete. Rubbing
the one fact against the other, his superiors were pleased
to reward him with exile, assigning him to a French
battalion. In this way, the army deals with a chronic
shortage: In French Switzerland, there are not enough
officers to go around, not enough people who are willing
to pay the grade, so the army must fill in with Swiss
Germans. He said he had once been part of a Tenth
Division company in which every officer was a Suisse
allemand. There was contentment in his face and a
playful smile as he completed this discussion. He said,
"The French Swiss Army drinks wine, the German
Swiss Army almost never." And he finished his chocolate pear.

Major Jaussi said the pear was for officers only. He
called it "a little amelioration." The dinner had otherwise been served in various places to soldiers as well. I
learned somewhat later that it had been prepared by a
chef tournant from the brigade de cuisine of the Hotel
zum Storchen, in Zurich. His name was Fredi Eckert—
a tall, dark-haired twenty-seven-year-old cook with eyes
as dark brown as finishing chocolate. Until quite recently, he had been cooking at the Hyatt Regency in
Chicago. He had returned to Switzerland for the army
some weeks beforehand, so that he could take up his

new position at the Storchen and be paid his salary while off with the troops in the mountains. This was completely acceptable to the Storchen, whose general manager, Major Jean-Philippe Jaussi, would be in the same mountains at the same time, and in the same battalion, of which he is commanding officer. Jaussi had long known Corporal Eckert in the army, had employed him earlier at the Hotel zum Storchen, and had arranged his experiences in kitchens from Ticino to Vaud, in Nice, in Zurich, in Chicago. Jaussi regards his dual association with the chef as "typical of the importance of the army in civilian life." As chef tournant at the Storchen, Eckert had been working one day as saucier, the next as pâtissier, the next as garde-manger, and so on, amply proving to one and all that the hotel was fortunate to have him—not to mention the battalion, where his presence was more than a little amelioration. In this refresher course, in the battalion kitchen in the Val d'Anniviers, he had working under him as assistant cooks a biologist, an engineer, a baker, and a ship's officer from a boat on Lake Geneva. "I have always to look around," Eckert told me when I met him. "Sometimes they don't know how to take the knife in the hand."

Soldiers in refresher courses will typically eat in village restaurants, where they buy drinks but are served food that is carried into the restaurants by the army. Few battalions have a chef tournant as caporal de cuisine. On a table—serve yourself—there might be an army-colored ice chest full of lukewarm macaroni. A peck of oiled lettuce in a big aluminum pot. Some bread. Some cheese. No pears under chocolate sauce. The army kitchen staffs carry hot food wherever the soldiers happen to be. Rumpf and I were watching machine-gun practice one day, far up in the Saastal, several miles from the nearest road, in a thick snowstorm. The visibility could not have been more than three hundred feet. Around the white mountainside appeared a line of ice-bearded porters—looking for all the world like hired Sherpas—carrying brown ice chests full of hot carrots, rice, and stew.

Major Jaussi said that he was waiting for the sound of a helicopter. His mortar company was about to be inspected by the Commandant de Corps. The mortars had been set up a few miles away, and we would go there to meet the chopper. He spoke with enthusiasm about the usefulness of mortars. "For me, as battalion commander, they are my little artillery. They are precise. They are mobile, not too heavy. They cover three and a half to four kilometres. In the mountains, that is good. You can shoot from one valley to the other."

Thirty years ago, this same battalion—the Seventh Battalion of the Fifth Regiment of the Tenth Mountain Division—was commanded by Major Jaussi's father, Major Jaussi. If the present Major Jaussi were to win an international prize, I doubt that he would regard the fact with more affection. "In certain families," he said, "being in the Mountain Corps is a very strong tradition." In days that followed, I would come to know him, to talk with him at greater length than in the old schoolhouse in Mission, and he told me that when his father was not serving in the army he was being trained at the Meurice, in Paris, the Dorchester, in London, for the family has traditions in the hotel business, too, in both French and German Switzerland, reaching back through six generations. In 1969, Jean-Philippe Jaussi went to Cornell, for a semester at the school of hotel management, and in Ithaca, America, he found a truly novel world. "People said, 'Pop in. Pop in.' Wherever I went in America, people would say, 'Pop in. Pop in.' This American expression changed my approach to life. In Switzerland, it is impossible. Unimaginable. No one says, 'Pop in.' Or anything like it. My family had a big house in the country between Vevey and Montreux, about a mile back from the lake. If we wished to have visitors, my mother was always asking a week's notice. She would clean all the windows. Everything had to be perfect—the Swiss way. It's a little heavy. The Swiss are too well educated, a little too stiff, while the American says, 'Just pop in. You know where the fridge is. Just help yourself.' "

"Not this American," I murmured, zipping up my army cardigan against a mountain draft.

"If you speak French in German Switzerland, it is hard to get along, hard to make friends," Jaussi said. "Ithaca was a friendly, open world. At Cornell, they think Swiss are Swedes. Cornell never heard of Switzerland."

Jaussi had worked at the Waldorf-Astoria—and the Greenbrier, in White Sulphur Springs, West Virginia. "The Waldorf was a world in itself, a little city with people walking through the lobby, going from Park to Lex. It was like a bee house. In Switzerland, after midnight, there is not much going on. New York never ends. It is on a twenty-four-hour basis. I went everywhere—to Broadway, to the ballet, the Village Vanguard, Harlem. I was squeezing the lemon. I lived on

Eighty-first between Lex and Third. The Greenbrier, like the Peninsula Hotel, in Hong Kong, was run by a Swiss Mafia. Hermann Rusch, the Swiss chef, was there. Virtually all the key positions were Swiss. It was a resort lost in the middle of nowhere, with a village living on the hotel. A truck went to New York for goods twice a week. I worked under Rusch as garde-manger, among ice carvings and butter sculptures. I met Sam Snead."

Returning to Switzerland, he had applied for a job at the Hotel Zurich, and had made clear to his prospective employers his lifelong dual ambition: to manage a first-class hotel and to take the time as well to try to become an army major, to "match the achievement" of his father. He had every reason to suspect that his plan would be regarded with favor, because the Hotel Zurich —like the Hotel zum Storchen—was owned by Oerlikon-Bührle, a diversified company that manufactures (among other things) anti-aircraft guns, armored personnel carriers, and missile launchers, and has as its chief executive officer Colonel Dieter Bührle, a member of the general staff. Hired to do sales and marketing, Jaussi went off to Milwaukee, to Albany, to Kansas City, successfully drumming up trade. He was surprised when the Hotel zum Storchen job was offered to him, because, as a Suisse romand, he felt himself a bit of a foreigner in La Suisse Allemande. To run the hotel by the river in the old city—where Paracelsus had been a guest, as had Richard Wagner—he thought the company would want a Zuricher, with Zurich dialect, when all he could speak was High German. He was chosen because he was a captain in the army. It was simply "a matter of leadership." The Storchen has a cloistered arcade, a boat

"Before they shoot, what do they do to make sure it's safe?" I asked.

Captain Rumpf said, "They go to church."

Franchini polled the mortar crews, asking what they did "in life." They were cheesemakers, boat builders, masons, farmers. In shifting the mortars around, they had turned away from a short high view of the snowy Dent Blanche and other Pennine summits to a distant picture of the Bernese Oberland framed in the steep green valley, with its chalets and meadows, its snowfields and forest. Franchini had not come for the view. He had singled out a corporal for particular instruction, informing him that his retreating manner and lack of bearing were at least as disturbing as his ignorance of mortars.

The corporal was nervous. He said, "Oui, mon Divisionnaire."

Franchini said, "Je suis le Commandant de Corps." Speaking further about the need for firm base plates, he asked, as he finished, "Compris?"

The corporal said, "Compris, Divisionnaire."

Franchini said. "Je suis le Commandant de Corps." He mentioned to the corporal that he would be a more effective leader if he stood up straight. Did the corporal agree?

"Oui, oui, Divisionnaire."

"Commandant de Corps!"

Franchini tended to gesture with his hands. Like a maestro, he moved them up and down. In one famous moment, when he was in a similar discussion with a rattled soldier, the soldier misinterpreted the gestures, reached out, and warmly shook Franchini's hand. This corporal, however, kept his arms at his sides, and did not seem to be thinking that he had made a new friend.

"A day without adequate preparation is a day lost," Franchini was saying. Did the corporal understand?

The corporal said, "Compris, Divisionnaire."

Gently, the Commandant said, "Je suis le Commandant de Corps."

"Compris," said the corporal.

If the corporal did not know what he was doing, he could not possibly lead others. Was that understood?

"Compris."

If he did not suggest in his own bearing a sense of purpose and pride, all discipline would disintegrate beneath him. Was that understood?

"Compris. Compris."

If the base plate were to shift in the ground, the shell could end up in the battalion's headquarters. Was that clear enough?

"Compris. Compris."

Service compris.

"Fermez les bouteilles!" barked Massy, in his voice of mock command. After the flag ceremony, he and his company were served stew in the meadow where they had left their packs, and now it was time to move—to climb about a thousand feet to their quarters, in Ried, a village said by Lieutenant Wyssa to be a ninety-minute walk from Brig. Massy was by no means the only soldier who had brought wine for the noonday meal, but he alone had brought a glass. The others drank from their bottles. A hundred and thirty speckled gray packs were lined up in neat rows, like granite tombstones, near the joking, reuniting soldiers, whose automatic rifles were resting on their bipods by the packs. A soldier with an apple in his hand was sleeping on the ground. For a time, he went on sleeping while the rest of the company stirred.

Before long, Lieutenant Wyssa gave an order a good deal more official than "Fermez les bouteilles." The Section de Renseignements, moving out past the marble yard and the remorseless Toyota forklift, ambled in a southerly direction through the fringes of the town. As before, they did not march; they walked—single file or double or triple, at the soldiers' choice. "Serrez! Serrez!" Wyssa called out, trying to keep them together, for they tended to be vague, like strollers on an evening paseo instead of a typical Swiss infantry unit demonstrating its precision and anticipatory responses to command. "Serrez! Serrez!"

Even within the limits of Brig, there were Brown Swiss cows and black-nosed Valais sheep. There were stone barns. I asked the agronomist Jean-Bruno Wettstein if—as in the high alpages—the little barns were called écuries.

"In the French part of Switzerland, we don't speak French very well," he said. "Actually, an écurie is for horses, and an étable is for cows. The Swiss mix the terms. They use them interchangeably. If a place has room for animals and people, it is called a chalet d'alpage."

We moved under a road sign that said "SIMPLON ITALIA," and soon left the road to walk beside a stream. It was called the Saltina, and it came from the mountains around Simplon Pass. Rushing white, it was having a last word before expiring into the Rhone. The soldier walking in front of me could not hear the noisy water. He had earphones in his ears, and the wires ran inside his mountain jacket. "In the Section de Renseignements, we try to decide what is the intention of the enemy," Lieutenant Wyssa said to me, in a voice pitched high to ride over the sound of the stream. "We seek information, and sometimes it seeks us. Before we can use it, we must decide if it is true, probable, or false." I asked him what he had studied at Penn, and he said, "Anti-trust and tax law."

Leaving the Saltina, the soldiers climbed a short, steep trail through woods and reached a road that doubled back to a high stone bridge across the stream. It was called Napoleon's Bridge, and Napoleon was said to have crossed it with an army at some point on the road to Elba. The soldiers were quoting Napoleon: "Les meilleures troupes, celles auxquelles vous pouvez faire le plus confiance, ce sont les Suisses!" A Valais mercenary battalion worked for Napoleon in Spain and Russia.

"The French people are not rid of him yet," said Jean-Bruno Wettstein.

The bridge spanned a gorge that no terrestrial vehicle could cross on its own. Small steel doors in one pier hinted that Napoleonsbrücke was ready to blow. It had been superseded, however, by an even higher bridge, which leaped through the sky above—a part of the new road to Simplon. In an extreme emergency, the midspan of the new bridge would no doubt drop on the old one.

Set back on the flaring lip of the gorge was a spread of numbered squares: 1, 2, 3, 4, 5, 6—a three-hundred-metre target range. One sees such ranges near every village and town: against rock outcrops, across meadows as smooth and green as cricket pitches, halfway up hillsides backstopped with forest. Shooting rifles is a national sport. It is also compulsory. The national shooting contests—the Knabenschiessen, the Wyberschiessen, the Rütlischiessen—are major annual events, even more important than the Steinstossen, in which the object is to heave as far as possible a rock that weighs a hundred and eighty-four pounds. (The Swiss—and therefore world—record is three and a half metres.) Meanwhile, soldiers in all age groups practice at their local shooting ranges and must demonstrate adequate competence once a year. Massy goes to the range up the hill behind Epesses; Wettstein goes down the road from Nyon to targets set up close to the French frontier. In their annual test, they fire twenty-four shots, some rapidly, some at will, against plain and camouflaged targets. There is a point system, with a perfect score of a hundred and twelve. If they fail to score fifty-two, they have to put on their uniforms and report to Lausanne for two days of shooting under instructive supervision.

Wettstein said, "I score in the sixties. I'm not a very good shooter, even if I try. Once, I did well. I had a ninety-one."

"You closed your eyes and had a lucky day."

"No. My brother went for me."

"Serrez! Serrez!"

One of Wettstein's childhood heroes was the runner Jean-François Pahud. When Wettstein spent his year at Linn-Mar High School, in Marion, Iowa, he was a middle- and long-distance running star. So impressed are the Swiss with the accomplishments of Swiss in the United States that the entire top floor of the Musée des Suisses à l'Étranger, outside Geneva, is given over to the subject. There is a lovingly framed photograph of the basketball team of Berne High School, in Indiana. There are snapshots, newspaper pages, and so forth Switzerland County, Indiana; Tell City, Indiana; New

Bern, North Carolina; East Bernstadt, Kentucky; New Glarus, Wisconsin. There are testimonials to the families from Ticino who emigrated to Asti, California, and made Italian Swiss Colony wine.

An oil portrait of General Johann August Sutter, of Basel, presents him with a broad-brimmed flat-topped hat above crafty blue eyes and a gray handlebar mustache—looking much like, and even less military than, Harland Sanders, of Kentucky, the chicken colonel. Sutter, of course, was a general nowhere, least of all in Switzerland—but he founded New Helvetia, California, whose name became Sacramento after gold was discovered there, in 1848.

Portraits and paraphernalia of the most major figures march down the walls of the museum's attic rooms.

Albert Gallatin, of Geneva, instructor in French at Harvard, United States representative, United States senator, Secretary of the Treasury at the time of the Louisiana Purchase.

Louis Agassiz, of Neuchâtel, one of the most celebrated professors Harvard has ever had, who convinced the world of the validity of his theory that ice two miles thick had once spread widely over Europe and North America.

William Wyler, of Oberehrendingen, in the Canton d'Argovie, director of "Wuthering Heights," director of "Friendly Persuasion," director of "The Big Country," director of "Ben Hur."

Louis Chevrolet, of La Chaux-de-Fonds, Canton de Neuchâtel, who emigrated to the United States at the age of twenty-one, undertook to make motor vehicles, and placed on the front end of each of them the enduring emblem that "n'est pas sans rappeler, de façon stylisée, le pays d'origine du constructeur"—that is, the map of Switzerland.

Othmar-Hermann Ammann, of Schaffhausen, civil engineer, variously designer or builder of the Golden Gate Bridge, the Verrazano-Narrows Bridge, the Hell Gate Bridge, the Queensboro Bridge, the Triborough Bridge, the Throgs Neck Bridge, the Bronx-Whitestone Bridge, the Goethals Bridge, the Bayonne Bridge, the George Washington Bridge, the Lincoln Tunnel.

So proud is Switzerland of its progeny in America that mention is made even of Solomon Guggenheim, who was born in Philadelphia to parents born in Switzerland.

"Serrez! Serrez!"

The stragglers coalesced beyond Napoleon's Bridge.

Soon we were looking far down on Brig from high rural ground, a breeze in our faces, the Saltina delta and the Rhone Valley deep in the lee of the Bernese Oberland. Turning the other way, we faced the Hübschhorn, all white and half in sunlight up the pass. Wettstein said that while the Simplon Tunnel was being built, before the First World War, the army attacked striking workers. In 1932, when there were political riots in Geneva, the army killed thirteen civilians and wounded eighty. "The army defends against the enemy and preserves internal peace." He also said that the public rampage of recent times by discontented youth had become "minor, small scale," and was "not representative of Switzerland; young Swiss today have become conservative and less absorbed with politics, as they have in the States."

We went by small farms with block-lettered messages on the farmhouse walls beseeching God to guard them. We passed cherry trees that were now as orange as maples. There were more black-nosed sheep, and, at every turn, the universal cattle, with the tintinnabulation of their bells, bells, bells—the clink and clank and clangor of the bells.

A chalet under construction irritated Wettstein. "These are hay meadows," he said. "And there is a problem if they are used for construction. In the mountains, there is plenty of room for grazing but not enough for hay." Since the Second World War, in a steady attrition, Switzerland has lost to development nearly forty per cent of its productive agricultural land. When Wettstein was ten years old, he decided he wanted to be a farmer; but in Switzerland—as an expression goes—it is more difficult to become a farmer than to become President of the Confederation. A farm of, say, sixty acres would cost more than a million dollars if it were available, and that is unlikely. Wettstein settled for agronomy. To the south of us, beyond the Hübschhorn, he had worked not long before at a chalet d'alpage that sends milk plunging by pipeline three kilometres to the village of Simplon, where it is made into cheese—assuming it is not butter when it arrives. Describing the operation, Wettstein quoted J. Robert Oppenheimer on the development of the fission bomb, saying it was one per cent genius and ninety-nine per cent hard work. Wettstein has also put in some months trying to improve the deteriorating chalets and bad grass of Bourg-Saint-Pierre, near the Grand-Saint-Bernard Pass. At Vernamiège, high up the side of the Val d'Hérens, he cleaned up the overgrowth on abandoned agricultural terraces—restoring the land, removing the fire danger, and kicking out the vipers.

"The . . . ?"

"Snakes. They are poisonous adders. They are all over Switzerland. They are not good for tourists. There are many in Valais—everywhere up to two thousand metres."

"What is our present altitude?"

"Eight hundred metres. They don't bite much. You have to step on them. No one is killed by them. They are mostly dangerous to children."

We walked by small perfect squares of standing corn, tan now and dry, stiff as hairbrushes among the grazed meadows. We walked by huge cabbages. Wettstein said, "Children in Switzerland are born in cabbages, so the cabbages must be large."

And eighty-nine minutes after the climb to Ried began, the Section de Renseignements arrived in the center of the village. "Eighty-nine minutes," said Massy. "Lieutenant Wyssa told us ninety. He doesn't lie too much."

It was a village of small homes and a few granaries standing on posts interrupted by broad discs of rock, keeping rodents away from the grain—a simple mountain town no larger than Epesses, and not nearly as compact and ornate. Incongruous in its center was a dark-wood-and-concrete modern school. It sat on a foundation so generously poured that the building seemed to be about two-thirds basement. A large L-shaped entryway led into the basement. A sentry with rifle stood at the bend in the L. Most of the soldiers waited outside—waited to be issued more clothing, extra gear. A swarm of farmers in uniform—who are known as soldats du train because they deal with horses—were singing and swilling in groups. One after another, the Vaudois soldiers went up to the village bulletin board and squinted at a language they could not read. "They discover the geography of Switzerland," said Corporal Philip Müheim, who works in an import-export office in Vevey. "This army is more human than military. We are militarily ten or fifteen years behind, but the army is a tradition." The Swiss school system tends to separate people from the age of twelve according to background, intelligence, and future profession. In the vital way that the American public high school draws together the skeins of American society, the Swiss Army knits Switzerland.

Wettstein said, "If an enemy comes, the whole thing will be over blitzkrieg fast."

Dark was coming on, and the air was cold. When at last it was time to go inside, Massy and the others carried their gear past the sentry in the doorway and went in under the school. The basement door, standing open, was nearly two feet thick and was made of concrete framed with steel. Its hinges were like cannon barrels. Inside were rooms enough—room after room after room—to contain the population of the town. Latrine, showers, kitchen—all of it was under a concrete ceiling three feet thick. It was not the fate of the Section de Renseignements to sleep in a room near the door—to have whatever advantage such propinquity might provide. They had been assigned to a room beyond a room —blank-walled, with sixteen double bunks filling up most of the space, foam mattresses on the bunks. Massy climbed to an upper bunk and sat there looking depressed, with his legs dangling. In bunks around and below him were Pillard, Wettstein, Tanniger, Layaz, Schyrr, Pera. After unrolling a towel, Massy slowly elevated the cork in a bottle of Clos du Boux Epesses. He looked dismally around the gray walls of the village bomb shelter. His glance was arrested by a long galvanized tube suspended like stovepipe from the ceiling and designed to bring in fresh air. Lugubriously, he said, "La fenêtre."

There was a two-centi-litre pause between "la" and "fenêtre." Massy poured a taste of wine. To come into the army, he had left his cave, and now he was back in a cave. Soldiers unpacked, stretched out, dealt cards. Massy passed the glass to the right, and jumped down from his bunk. He had noticed in the rear wall a small steel door secured with large levers, like a hatch in a submarine. He lifted the levers and, with considerable effort, swung the door open. It was about three feet by two, and nine inches thick, and weighed at least six hundred pounds. On the other side was empty darkness. Without so much as putting on a yellow slicker, Massy entered this cuve of cuves. Not for nothing was he in Renseignements. He vanished into the darkness. There were sounds of upward scuffle. Soon he came back down. His head appeared in the hatchway. "Trees! I saw living trees!" he said. "It is the emergency escape. There is a way out of here. We can leave after lights!"

During the Second World War, as the Swiss observed the destruction of cities around them, they had no difficulty imagining such scenes transposed to Switzerland. They were particularly alarmed by the firestorms that killed large percentages of the civilian populations of places like Hamburg and Dresden, and they set out to learn what they could about how to prevent a similar devastation of Zurich. After the war, they sought out as a consultant a former Nazi major general who had commanded fourteen thousand soldiers fighting fires in Berlin. They learned, among other things, that the civilians of the German cities had roasted to death in basements that were swept over by fires moving from one to another of the lightly constructed buildings above—deaths that might not have occurred within walls and ceilings made of thick concrete.

In the late nineteen-forties, Swiss people building private homes and apartment houses voluntarily used such construction. In the fifties came subsidies and regulation—the forty-centimetre concrete ceiling—but still the official purpose was to protect the population from destruction such as had occurred in Europe during the Second World War. Not until twenty years after Hiroshima did Switzerland shift its attention to the Third World War and begin to design shelters against the effects of nuclear weapons. The Swiss in the nineteen-sixties had no idea what such a program would cost, nor did they attempt to work out a cost-benefit ratio, because they saw the benefit as both imperative and infinite, and therefore inexpressible in arithmetical terms. The author Jonathan Schell, writing in a different and wider context, recently expressed the Swiss point of view exactly when he said, "A society that systematically shuts its eyes to an urgent peril to its physical survival and fails to take any steps to save itself cannot be called psychologically well."

After studying Samuel Glasstone on "The Effects of Nuclear Weapons," and all related unclassified material, the Swiss eventually settled on the concept of the one-bar shelter. A bar is a unit of pressure—of the sort that explosions make—and is equivalent to ten metric tons per square metre. Walls and ceilings can be built to withstand such pressure. Close to a nuclear explosion, pressures are of course much higher, and in that zone people in one-bar shelters would be lost, but as the pressure wave spreads, it declines rapidly. At Hiroshima, a one-bar shelter might have saved lives half a mile from the bomb. At Nagasaki, too. The pressure wave from a hundred-kiloton bomb (five times the size of Nagasaki's) would decline to one bar in somewhat under a mile. One megaton—two and six-tenths kilometres. Two megatons —four kilometres. Five megatons—five and a half kilometres. Twenty megatons—eight kilometres. Very few warheads are as large as that.

Conceding general destruction on the closer ground —and assuming bombs exploding anywhere—the Swiss started building one-bar shelters to protect the extremely high percentage of the population that might survive explosions but without shelter would be destroyed like the citizens of Hamburg and Dresden. Swiss calculations showed that something as thick as, say, a ten-bar shelter would be of negligible extra value, for the increased area of protection would be slight rather than proportional; for underground hospitals and command posts, three-bar construction was chosen. Light and heat from a nuclear explosion that would blind and severely burn a person who happened to be outdoors would at the same distance have no effect on a person in a one-bar shelter. Arriving with and soon after the light would be gamma rays and neutrons—radiation against which the shelters must include adequate shielding. Water is adequate, and there is a good deal of it in concrete. Early fallout, downwind, occurs through twenty-four hours—and arrives in pieces as large as coins, ranging on down to dust. If the pieces are sucked in by shelter ventilators, they are stopped by filters.

Particles emitting radiation also cling to dust that hovers at high altitudes or travels around the planet and when it falls cannot penetrate a one-bar shelter. Civil-defense experts of various countries agree that two weeks in the shelter will cover the worst possibilities of delayed fallout. But—as a civil-defense engineer once explained to me in Bern—"even when radiation is down, it is still high by peacetime standards; you do not go out and walk with the children." His name was Friedrich Sager, and he was vice-director of Swiss civil defense, in charge of all household shelters, including the large ones, such as Massy's military bedroom. "One hour after the explosion, you go out and measure the intensity of the radiation," Sager went on. "If it is very high, you go back in. After two days, it will have decreased a hundred times. An explosion in a nearby country could be a serious fallout problem. Neutrality helps not at all. After one or two days, you can go upstairs—assuming there is an upstairs —take a bath, feed the pet. If you have previously closed all doors and windows, you will have minimum particles in the house and none in the shelter. So this gives you an opportunity to make a warm meal, take care of the little doggy—it's only a matter of time, O.K.?—and then get back into the shelter. You stay in the shelter as long as you can. Three weeks, if you can. In a good shelter, you can say, 'My home is my castle.'"

Water is more important than food, he pointed out. And, like air, water that is exposed to radiation does not become radioactive and can be filtered. On this matter, out of curiosity as much as anything else, Swiss civil-defense officials asked their English counterparts how much water Lord Nelson carried on his warships. The answer was less than four litres per day per man. In all shelters, from private ones in houses to big ones sleeping whole towns, people are supposed to supply their own food. "First, they bring their fat," Sager said. "They can live on that for at least a week. The average household keeps food enough on hand. There are no requirements for stocking shelters." Anyone who has built a house in recent decades has, by force of law, a shelter at home, usually full of ski boots and wine. All over Switzerland, one sees schools and public buildings resting like the tips of icebergs on their enormous one-bar basements. All over Switzerland, in relatively spacious and quiet towns, are sophisticated underground parking garages with automatic machines that offer tickets like tongues and imply a level of commerce that is somewhere else. In a nuclear emergency, huge doors would slide closed with the town's population inside. In the charming old sections of cities, with their astigmatic windows, and timbers that creak like wooden ships, no effort has been made to add shelters under the buildings. Big public shelters have been developed instead. There is a garage in Zurich that is ready for seven thousand people. The biggest bomb shelter in the world is the Sonnenberg Tunnel, in which an Autobahn traverses Lucerne. In a nuclear emergency, doors high enough and wide enough for the hangar of a rigid airship would slide on rails and close the tunnel. Made of tessellated slabs of concrete, the doors are five feet thick. There is a command post inside, and a hospital, and sleeping accommodations for twenty thousand people. Environmentalists are at present attempting to prevent the construction of an Autobahn tunnel through the Bernese Oberland. A friend in Basel once said to me, "If environmentalists had been around a hundred years ago, there would now be no place to hide."

"The principal remaining problem is to shelter small clustered rural communities, but farmers will never build shelters," Sager told me. "They are thinking in litres of milk. The only solution is higher subsidies. Epesses? You never touch such a village with shelters. It is too beautiful. Instead, put a big hole in the ground. Persuade the people to keep their wine there. Epesses today has almost no shelters. In peacetime, they could use one not only for storage but for drinking and eating, too. They could enjoy themselves. How is it they call such a cellar? Ah—a carnotzet."

To be informed about radiation levels, direction of fallout, and the progress of war, any shelter large or small wants to be in close communication with a command post. Civil-defense command posts are meant to cover about twenty thousand people. Sager took me into one below a firehouse near Bern—a three-bar shelter fourteen feet deep, with outer walls twenty inches thick. We went down a narrow flight of stairs into an airlock, then into a room with two showers, and then into a dozen more rooms, glistening clean, with many rows of telephones, electronic equipment, telecommunications equipment, triple-deck bunks, a stocked kitchen, a diesel generator, and twenty-four hundred litres of diesel fuel—all in place, ready. In the conference-and-recreation room, a large mural had been painted by visiting schoolchildren—a primitive in primary colors—of cable cars and boats, castles and balloons, Swiss cities and country, Swiss mountains and the moon. There was a blackboard on which someone had written these words exactly: "McKill-Roy Is Watching You."

Such a deep token of preparedness implies a deeper history of threat. From the joining of the first three cantons to the army maneuvers of the present day, Switzerland has existed to repel offensive neighbors, and with regard to this subject has never felt complacent or relaxed. It would be very un-Swiss to wake up tomorrow to yesterday's threat and then attempt to do something about it. If Pearl Harbor had somehow been in Switzerland, a great deal of Japanese aluminum would be scattered all over the Alps. Never in modern times, of course, has threat to Switzerland been more continuous than from 1939 to 1945, and while underground command posts with walls as thick as Dunsinane's may have been designed in the nineteen-seventies according to the science of nuclear-weapons effects, they are also hidden monuments to the anxieties of the Second World War.

While actual battles were being fought to the west, the north, the south, the east, simulated battles were taking place inside Switzerland. To keep itself prepared, and abreast of new technologies, the Swiss Army imitated the war that was going on around it. During the siege of Stalingrad, during the desert campaign, during the invasion of Sicily and the Battle of the Bulge, Swiss soldiers in Switzerland were firing weapons identical or equivalent to the weapons then in use in the war. They were fording rivers in full battle dress, stringing barbed wire, bivouacking in deep winter snows, scrubbing their laundry in summer streams, climbing rock faces with machine-gun parts, hauling cannons into high alpages. They were always on patrol—on skis, on foot, on motorcycles, on bicycles, in boats.

Now and then, they shot down a trespassing aircraft. Other planes, damaged, requested and received permission to land. Some, abandoned by pilots and crews, just drifted into Switzerland and crashed. An empty American B-17 hit a medieval castle and filled its tall tower with flaming gasoline. A Red Cross library on international peace had been put in the tower so that it would not be damaged in the war. Imagining themselves to be over Germany, twenty American bombers dropped four hundred bombs on Schaffhausen, Switzerland's northernmost city. A German plane carrying an experimental package of supersecret radar made an unintentional landing near Zurich, possibly guided by the supersecret radar. The Swiss seized the radar and hid it in an alp. The Nazis threatened invasion. The Swiss offered a deal. They brought the radar out of the alp and destroyed it in the presence of German witnesses in return for a dozen fighter planes, on which the iron crosses were repainted white.

Early in the war, as the rest of Europe blacked out,

Switzerland still sparkled with light and served as a beacon to aircraft of any description. The Germans were particularly uncomfortable with this flashlight at their side. They told Switzerland to shut off the light or Germans would come and do it for them. Switzerland went dark. Switzerland had mobilized when Germany invaded Poland. The Swiss imagined that their turn was coming, too. In months that followed, as fear of invasion temporarily declined, many men were sent home "on leave" —each with his gun and forty-eight bullets—only to be called back when Germany invaded France, Luxembourg, Belgium, and Holland. Motion pictures were stopped in mid-performance. Announcements were read. Swiss soldiers were ordered straight out of the cinemas and into the field. Mobilization, always rapid, expanded with each successive threat and declined soon afterward. Whenever things looked bad, more than four hundred thousand Swiss soldiers were at their battle stations. Things looked bad when Germany piled up beside the Bodensee enough munitions, matériel, and implied manpower to relocate Switzerland in Sardinia. At times like these, there was some panic. A significant piece of the population of Basel departed. At least two thousand never came back. Cars streamed across the country with mattresses on their roofs to absorb possible bullets from the air. The pile of matériel by the Bodensee turned out to be a ruse to divert attention from an attack in preparation elsewhere. In 1940, the Germans and the Italians actually did form a plan to attack Switzerland. The Germans meant to take Geneva from France and then cross the Mittelland to Bern. They would also come down past Basel to Lucerne. Meanwhile, the Italian

Army was assigned to capture the Alps. The German code name for all this was Tannenbaum. The plan included a map of the Axis apportionment of Swiss territory. The Germans were to get the Mittelland, the Italians the rocks.

The Swiss knew nothing of Tannenbaum. But they imagined something like it. Paintings and stained-glass windows went into storage underground. From time to time, attack was not just feared but anticipated. When German armies entered Denmark and Norway, the Swiss expected them to come south as well. After France was gone, rationing became general, and eventually included such things as pet food and flour and (perhaps worst of all) chocolate, but by neighboring standards the rationing was not severe: the people were denied meat two days a week. Also after France surrendered, the German military attaché sought out Jakob Huber, the Swiss chief of the general staff, and made it clear that he felt the time had come for Switzerland to open its doors and welcome a German Europe. There was a six-decilitre pause. Huber studied the attaché and said, "No one comes through here."

Some things did go through here, however—in sealed trains. People wondered what was inside. When coal trains went through, no one could see what was under the coal. By the terms of a 1909 treaty, the coal itself was permissible, as were wheat, oil, timber, steel— all of which went through Switzerland on the way from Germany to Italy. The trains came back with vegetables. For Switzerland to permit war matériel to pass through Switzerland would have been an abdication of neutrality: no less a deception than if Henri Guisan were to dress as a civilian and ride a train out of Switzerland to strengthen his connections with the French—as he did, not long before the outbreak of war. Switzerland played both sides for the middle. For the Allies, the Swiss manufactured ball bearings, jewel bearings, theodolites, chronographs, machine tools. In 1941, under German pressure, the Swiss government decreed that packages could not be sent abroad, thus cutting off shipments of small precision parts to Britain. For the Axis, the Swiss made fuses, timed as fine as clocks. They made ball bearings for the Nazis, too. In June of 1943, the British dropped a few bombs into an industrial section of Zurich —a message in exploding code. When the Swiss Army learned of German plans to assassinate General Dwight Eisenhower and General Jean de Lattre de Tassigny, they described the plans to the Americans and the French.

As Switzerland was subjected to various threats and pressures, particularly from the north, it was the art of General Guisan to bend just enough to avoid fracture, to grant an hour to gain a day, to sell a little something but not to sell out. He was a Vaudois farmer—a Suisse romand who openly detested the Nazis of Germany, and he was in charge of a nation in which a dismaying minority did not share that view. While his military task was to train his army and hold it ready to fight, his political objective was to dissuade all the people who were prepared to accept a German Europe, and his social goal was to rally the Swiss, to quell their fear, to replace their sense of helplessness with a sense of de-fensive strength—to keep the mattresses off the roofs of the cars. Canton to canton, he travelled the country, making his presence felt, urging soldiers and civilians to "Act Swiss! Think Swiss!" He said, "Switzerland can only avoid the threat of a direct German attack if the German high command, while preparing such an attack, becomes convinced that a war against us would be long and costly, that it would create a new battleground in the heart of Europe, in a most useless and dangerous way, and thus jeopardize the realization of its other plans." Accordingly, he advertised the preparedness of the army. He tried to toughen Switzerland internally while causing Switzerland to look tough from the outside. Given the will, the wherewithal, and the mountains, he said, the Swiss can keep anyone out. He made it absolutely clear to the Germans that if they invaded Switzerland the first thing they would hear would be a concerto of explosions as Switzerland's strategic railroads effectively ceased to exist. Highway bridges would be gone in the same moment. The knowledge of Switzerland's prepared demolition brought German saboteurs, who came to cut the wires, preceded by German spies. They had to be good to get to the wires or they found themselves in le trou. American, Russian, British spies—so many spies were in Switzerland during the war that they moved like slips of paper in a stock exchange. They were from every country but San Marino. Variously, they were spying on Switzerland, spying on one another, and using Switzerland as a telephone booth in which to report what they had been doing elsewhere. They met by matchlight under the dark arcades of Bern. Among them were Swiss. Fifteen Swiss traitors were executed during the war, most of whom were in the army. After they were sentenced, they were almost immediately killed by firing squads from their own army units.

Swiss schoolchildren are taught that Germany decided not to invade Switzerland because Germany knew that its losses would be too great—in what has become the classic phrase, "the price was too high."

"The Germans invaded the Dutch. The Dutch had declared themselves neutral. The Germans didn't come here, because of the Swiss Army."

"That's what I was taught in school. But then I have heard that it's not so simple."

"Did Switzerland avoid war as a result of the strategy of the great powers or the policy of neutrality or the strength of the army? We'll never know."

Near the end of the war, the Swiss went into mobilization one last time, because they foresaw a desperate Germany coming in to make defensive use of Swiss communications, and they also worried that the Allies might come through on their way to Germany. If these events had happened, the Swiss insist, they would have engaged in the war, fighting against both sides. In fact, Joseph Stalin did propose an Allied rampage through Switzerland, ostensibly en route to the evident enemy. Stalin hated the Swiss. He called them "swine." A month or two after his proposal, and perhaps by way of reply, Winston Churchill wrote to Anthony Eden: "I put this down for record. Of all the neutrals Switzerland has the greatest right to distinction. She has been the sole international force linking the hideously sundered nations and ourselves. What does it matter whether she has been able to give us the commercial advantages we desire or has given too many to the Germans, to keep herself alive? She has been a democratic state, standing for freedom in self-defence among her mountains, and in thought, in spite of race, largely on our side."

In August of 1945, in the square in front of the Ionic columns of the Curia Confoederationis Helveticae, in Bern, General Guisan stood before thousands of soldiers and civilians and received in formal ceremony their profound gratitude. The Swiss were celebrating the end of the war as if they had won it, and they had.

In late-evening darkness outside the bomb shelter in Ried, Captain Eric Dessemontet's Headquarters Company assembled in the town plaza and, in response to the captain's sharp commands, stood at something less than attention. There were those among them who swayed, leaned against one another, and occasionally broke into song. The plaza was essentially a wide spot in a small street. Automobiles kept arriving, and the soldiers had to break their ranks to let the cars go through. Called back into formation, they tended to huddle instead, noisily addressing one another while Dessemontet addressed them. "Taisez-vous!" he shouted, but they did not shut up. Between shouts, he said, sotto voce, to me, "I want you to know this is not unique. I always have this problem."

One might readily imagine that the problem was in the Section de Renseignements, but it was not. Within the assembled company, the Section de Renseignements stood quiet, at attention, and steady, like half a dozen rows of counted sheep. They may see themselves as headstrong, willful, insubordinate, but by comparison with the horse soldiers they are wimps to a man. Not only were the horse soldiers spackled out of their minds, they were also continuing to drink while they were meant to be standing at attention. They were farmers, for the most part—Vaudois farmers, from Rougemont and Château-d'Oex, towns en route from Montreux to Gstaad. For a farmer, going to the army can be less of a duty than a release, an only vacation, a celebration up the sides of the hills. An American colonel once told me, in careful words, that his impression of the Swiss Army was of "a different kind of discipline," of an order of magnitude "more relaxed than ours," but he added that in time of emergency such behavior would disappear. Even as the horse soldiers were flapping in formation like sheets in the wind, Massy remarked, "They are good, good people, the best we have."

The headlights of another automobile were slowly approaching through the standing ranks of soldiers. Some moved one way, some another to make a breach and let the car pass. The horse soldiers stayed put. They had been shouted at, cajoled, and told to stand still, and now they were not in a hurry to move for this car. From where I stood, the lights made silhouettes of them all— a black-on-gold unsteady tableau. Eventually, by ones and twos, they slowly moved aside, until only one soldier blocked the car—arms at his sides, chin tucked in, a body framed in headlights. One soldier, one automobile, one stalemate. Behind him, a booted foot lifted into the air, in silhouette moved slowly forward, and came to rest on the soldier's backside, centering on a spot eleven centimetres under the belt. The soldier was catapulted out of the scene, opening the way for the car.

Captain Rumpf and I went down one morning to see horses come off a train in Sierre. The army rents them from farmers. It is using three hundred in the present exercises, and this particular shipment was arriving from Winterthur. An owner had been up all night with the horses, in the cold and lurching freight cars, and now—dressed en bleu de travail—he looked not only tired but also intimidated as he presented his animals to Peter Keller. A doctor of veterinary medicine, Major Keller would decide if a horse was acceptable and—in case of accident—how much it was worth. Given his appearance, no one was likely to argue. Major Keller is a giant, an old-fashioned Swiss giant, in height, in frame, in voice, in beard, in motion—a giant. If he was not careful, he was going to knock over a freight car, and meanwhile he was looking down, with not unkindly eyes, upon this little wide-eyed farmer, who was scarcely five feet tall. The farmer led a horse down a ramp and, holding its halter, ran it up and down the cobblestone platform, his panting breath mixing with the steam from the nostrils of the horse.

"Thirty-two hundred," said Keller.

The owner looked relieved. Every horse, like every soldier, has its book of service, and this one's showed that it had first served the army three years ago. Its name was Barette. Others were Felix, Fauvette, Fleury, Flicka. They were big heavy draft horses reminiscent of the one beside the wall of Troy. As each horse gained Major Keller's approval, a soldier in knee-length boots and a ruddy camouflage jacket stepped up and led it away. The horse and the soldier would spend the entire refresher course together, going far up into the mountains beyond roads, up declivities beyond the grasp of four-wheel drive—the soldier walking, the horse in the traces of a two-wheeled pneumatic-tired cart full of rifles and personal gear and explosives, or food, or building materials, or bazookas, or ammunition, or hay. Officers ride. Soldiers walk. Among the soldiers was the usual preponderance of farmers, but there are not enough farmers anymore to match the number of horses, and also stepping forward to claim horses were a butcher, a mason, a painter of cars, a structural geologist, and an economist. The economist said he wished he could be in the cavalry, but this was all that was left. (He might have chosen bicycles. There are three bicycle regiments in the Swiss Army.) Horse and soldier would work and sleep in snowstorms. As a soldier led an animal away, sometimes both were hanging their heads.

"They walk and walk and walk," said Captain Rumpf. "The advantage is they don't need any petrol."

"Today, people laugh," said Major Keller. "Ultimately, we will have to go back to horses. Even now, when the weather is bad and the helicopters cannot fly, one is a hero to come into the mountains bringing supplies and hot food with horses."

There is no shortage of veterinarians in La Suisse Romande, but there is a shortage of veterinarians willing to give up the time to be officers, and since all army veterinarians must without exception be officers Major Keller has been borrowed from La Suisse Allemande. He works in toxicology for Hoffmann–La Roche, and may become a university professor. Only his habilitation stands in his way—a Germanic academic custom requiring as a condition of employment that a new professor have a completed and unpublished manuscript, by way of flooding instant credit upon the new employer. Albert Einstein, slow with his habilitation, worked in the patent office while waiting to teach at the University of Bern.

Peter Keller is a paradox of transportation. He deploys horses in the high Alps and in Montana rides Greyhound buses (stopping off to visit ranchers). In Switzerland, despite the national dimensions, he prefers most of all to fly. He is a pilot. On Sunday spins in rented Piper Archers, his routine is almost always the same—from Basel to the Bernese Oberland and across the Jungfraujoch divide, then over the Aletschgletscher and La Place de la Concorde Suisse, and then across the Rhone and up the Mattertal to circle the Matterhorn clockwise. Sometimes he lands in the Alps, in places so high, he says, "you need a good machine to get away with four people, otherwise they stick to the ground."

At the regimental headquarters one evening, Major Keller asked me if I had heard about the helicopter crash.

I said, "Yes. Last week in Grisons. What a shame. The pilot and the soldiers died."

He said, "Oh, no, not that one. I mean yesterday. Here in Wallis. It was another shame. There have been four accidents in the past week. Two jets. Two helicopters."

I said, "Peter, I am going to be spending a fair amount of time in helicopters, and right now I am eating my dinner."

He said, "They hit the wires. They always hit the wires. Sometimes farmers put up temporary wires and you cannot see them. Yesterday, again, the pilot and all the soldiers died. They had young children. They had children ten, twelve, fourteen years old."

At the Military Department in Bern, people were saying that there had actually been four and a half accidents. The half was a military policeman who fell off his motorcycle while escorting a foreign general.

Of one sort or another, there are a hundred thousand cables strung up the mountains of Switzerland. The country is a cat's cradle. One of the helicopter pilots was a forestry professor from Zurich flying five soldiers who were to play the role of enemy. Apparently blinded by the sun, the pilot hit a wire, and the helicopter fell into a gorge. The pilot had discussed that specific wire in the course of his preflight briefing. Meanwhile, a Swiss fighter pilot shot down another Swiss fighter pilot. The two were practicing. Making use of the Alps for military purposes in machines traveling near or beyond the speed of sound requires a great amount of practice— just to fly among the mountains, let alone to shoot.

"They can't miss one second. Otherwise, they run into a rock. They practice a lot. They also have a lot of accidents."

Airspace is so limited that some training is now done in Sweden, but there is only one place to practice flying in the Alps. The jet pilots fly low in the valleys and close to the rock. Nearly all Swissair pilots are in the Swiss Army's air force—and some doctors and dentists as well. They choose their own training time, and they need a good deal more than three weeks a year to learn

to do what they can do. The air force is an example of
contemporary technology demanding more time than a
militia is set up to provide. Like specialists in electronic
warfare, the pilots give extra time. When conditions
are what they want for practicing, they take their
Mirages, their Tigers, their Hunters and go. They develop incredible skill. They don't seem to use maps—
having so little glancing time, having every contour in
their heads. During the Second World War, after a
Swiss pilot shot down a German bomber over the
Canton de Neuchâtel the Germans sent fighters along
on a mission that deliberately traversed Swiss air. Swiss
pilots engaged the Luftwaffe in a dogfight and shot four
Germans down. Victors and vanquished were using
German airplanes. Swiss pilots now have infrared equipment and fly the mountain valleys at night. They can
hide in the Alps. They know where they are and where
to go. An enemy foolish enough to follow them will end
up farming rock. At Gornergrat one day, at the top of
a cog railway five thousand feet above Zermatt, I was
sitting in an almost windless stillness, slowly moving my
gaze in full circumference from the Breithorn to the
Matterhorn to the Dent Blanche to the Zinalrothorn to
the Weisshorn to the Dom—all well above four thousand metres—and on to the Dufourspitze, the highest
mountain in Switzerland. Up out of the Mattertal came
a Swiss Mirage. It skimmed over Gornergrat and dived
toward the glaciers below. Its inclination appeared almost vertical, and it continued its dive until there seemed
no chance that the plane could miss the ice and the pilot
survive, but then it was climbing the glaciers close to the
crevasses until it was deep in the cirques on the shoul-

ders of the Dufourspitze, over which it rolled to plunge out of sight toward the Mattmarksee. The pilot was probably taking pictures. Mirages work for Renseignements. The jets sometimes fire on targets and then, like high jumpers, flip over ridges upside down. It is a way to stay close to the rock. Their armament depends on their mission. Variously, they carry cannons, missiles, bombs. Even when cloud cover is extremely low during exercise engagements with the enemy, if someone calls for air support he will almost surely get it if there is any kind of airspace between the cloud and the ground. The Mirage drops out of the cloud, fires on the target, disappears upward in the cloud. It happens again a minute later. The target is destroyed twice. The cloud is packed like a snowfield among the Pennine Alps.

At Axalp, over the Brienzer See, the military attachés of at least twenty-five nations—including the United States, China, and the Soviet Union—sat down one day for a show. As the program began, a Mirage appeared from nowhere, rattled the reviewing stand, did a back flip over the Schwarzhorn, and was gone. Before the program ended, each attaché was handed a photograph of himself looking up with startled expression.

We have inched our way down the valleyside and taken the Nussbaum bridge—that is, taken notes on its width, its tonnage, its lack of prepared demolition. Beneath it is the bouldery Rhone, with long clear pools, short riffles and chutes. Among the renseignements the battalion needs to know is the answer to the question "Can the river be crossed here on foot?"

Massy sketches on paper the river, the bridge, and the flanking mountains. He says, conclusively, "It is possible to cross the Rhone on foot, but there is no advantage."

Jean-Bruno Wettstein says, "Massy has a great sense of strategy."

Denis Schyrr goes off to collect statistics on the Bettmeralp téléphérique. The others lean over the bridge parapet and fly-cast with their eyes. Trout rise. To pass the time, I remove from my mountain jacket my copy of "Armée Suisse." It is a paperback of small dimensions with a water-resistant cover, designed for a soldier's pocket. Words on the back say, "In the country of the citizen-soldier, 'Armée Suisse' is an indispensable book. It answers with precision all questions relative to the national defense." In three hundred and seventy-two pages of fine thin paper, it describes the organization, strategies, and equipment of the army, discusses rights, regulations, individual functions—all the basic facts a soldier should know. It is a semi-official volume, which is not given free to troops but is distributed through bookstores everywhere in Switzerland.

Wettstein asks, "What is the book you are reading?"

I hand it to him. He looks it over with considerable interest, having never seen one. The others crowd around like students around a yearbook. None of them has seen "Armée Suisse" before, although it has been in print for several years and is revised annually to keep the Swiss soldier up-to-date. On the back is a color photograph of a fusilier walking on the edge of a glacier, carrying a pack and wearing a steel helmet, his assault rifle suspended across his chest and his dagger hanging from his hip. Wettstein says, "There you have the Swiss soldier expressing his love of neutrality."

"Armée Suisse" has many photographs of Swiss equipment—from the F-5E Tiger to four kinds of grenades to tanks, bicycles, howitzers, and guided missiles—with accompanying statistics, such as weight and range and explosive charge. Much of the Swiss Army's equipment is American. Some is British, some French. Switzerland buys tank ammunition from Israel. Russians are distrustful of Swiss neutrality in part because Switzerland

buys nothing from them. The Swiss are militarily thrifty
—so much so that one would think at times that this is the
Scottish Army. While acquiring new wonders in infrared
vision, electronic deception, and computer warfare, they
continue to make use of equipment that is essentially
obsolete. Swiss pilots fly jets that are older than they are.
Until recently, Swiss paratroops jumped out of three
Junkers 52s, German transports from the Second World
War. The planes were wanted by museums all over
Europe, but they were not for sale. The army still uses
Centurion tanks that were made in Great Britain thirty
years ago. To keep such things in service is a tradition.
During the Second World War, there were Swiss artillery pieces on line and ready to fire which had been on
line and ready to fire since 1882. The Swiss throw nothing away, but their equipment is plenteous and for the
most part modern. They use McDonnell Douglas Dragon
rockets. Fifty years ago, when Swiss tank commanders
went out in the field for exercises they would say to
one another, "Shall we take three or all four?" Now
they have many tanks, if not as many as they think they
need. Most are state of the art and are made in Switzerland. The tanks do not yet have laser fire control, but
they will be acquiring it soon. The principal Swiss
artillery piece is a self-propelled howitzer made in the
United States. They call it "the American gun." To
increase the shooting distance, they have changed the
tube. Whether they design their own equipment or buy
it, they act with extreme care, always looking for sim-
plicity. They chose the F-5 over the F-16 because with
less difficulty they could keep it in the air.

The valley narrows where the river has cut a gorge.

La Place de la Concorde Suisse

At Grengiols, we cross a small bridge some two hundred feet above the water and follow a road chipped out of cliffs. Down the couloirs opposite, streams fall straight through forests under the skyline rock and on through green meadows to the Rhone. Farms are widely spread through the meadows. The rock above the tree line is largely covered with snow. The scene rises so steeply it seems painted on a curtain or a wall. From time to time, Haflingers, Pinzgauers, jeeps go by, providing glimpses of hats beribboned with gold. Officers ride. Soldiers walk. Up the road a few kilometres is Lax. The Major needs to know how large a military force could go past Lax without going through it. How much negotiable space is there in the level part of the valley? We will climb a thousand feet or so in order to form an opinion. The patrol will also choose a site for a new command post. Before attempting such a climb, they have thirst to be taken care of, and rest is called for, too. Close behind a small barn, in a meadow of purple dianthus, the patrol lies down. The barn is only a few metres wide but is an adequate screen from the Haflingers, Pinzgauers, and jeeps. It is written that no soldier out on patrol may go into a public building except on official business. So who will risk le trou to fetch some beer from Lax? Glances fly back and forth, cancelling one another out, until all eyes rest on the American observer.

A third of a mile from the barn, I find a market in the outskirts of town. I buy five litres of beer, and hold them like babies as I go back up the road. There is gratitude behind the barn, a certain something unspoken, too—a clear indication that, as General Guisan might put it, I have begun to think Swiss. I have earned my first cattle bell, and things look good for an oak-leaf cluster.

A boy happens by on a bicycle. Massy calls to him and offers him beer. Eagerly, he comes around the barn and drinks. He is seventeen, possibly. Most of his hair is dyed orange, and the remainder is Chinese red. As he drinks, an earring sways from one ear.

We climb now, away from the road, past a few houses and on into steep woods. Two small children come running out of a house and, following us, shout, "Bis . . . cuits! Bis . . . cuits! Bis . . . cuits!" By custom, kindly Swiss soldiers give cookies to kids. All we have to give them is beer. After a while, they abandon the chase, and their cries fade slowly behind us. "Bis . . . cuits! Bis . . . cuits!"

Lax is lovely from far above—a tall clock tower, an opulent ancient Valais town. Near a white church steeple, a lone maple blazes red-orange against a dark-green meadow. Renseignement: not much of an army could go past Lax without plowing through it. The valleysides are too abrupt. Far below us, among the chalets and barns, the cattle and meadows, we see rifles stacked outside tents, a dozen soldiers—no less expectable in a Swiss landscape than the ecclesiastical cows.

We descend obliquely through forest and pasture, cross the rails of the Furka-Oberalp, and continue up the Rhone. The light is falling as we go. It is dark when we reach the edge of Fiesch, with one more assignment to complete. There is a hydroelectric plant beside the river, but the water in the turbines is not from the Rhone. It comes from high in the Alps above, through a penstock drilled in the rock. The battalion needs to know the plant's capacity. It needs to know from exactly what place in the mountains the water descends. It needs to know if there are rungs or steps—some sort of cat-walk—in the penstock. But the hydroelectric plant is closed and dark. The air is cold now, and fanned by the fast-moving river. We are standing on a bridge leading to a locked door, and there is nothing to do but shiver.

Headlights turn toward us from the valley road. Miraculously, a Volkswagen Beetle descends to the power-plant bridge, crosses, parks; and a bearded man with a clipboard gets out and goes inside. Lights come on. The control room has tall plate-glass windows. We see him reading meters. Denis Schyrr and Pierre Pera follow him inside, but the engineer speaks no French and they speak no German. Of the five men in the patrol, only Jean-Bruno Wettstein speaks German. At the Swiss Federal Institute of Technology, in Zurich, he learned agronomy in German. Wettstein talks to the engineer. He learns that if a company of soldiers had to do it they could climb the mountain on the inside.

While Massy and the others are out on patrol, mortars pound the Mattertal, and the enemy is swept with pink tracers in the Val d'Anniviers. Soldiers with rifles and khaki rope belay down a cliff above Simplon Pass—hanging like spiders at the end of their silk. The Swiss forces are well spread out—each of the five companies in a battalion averaging, say, nine kilometres from the nearest of the four others, with the result that the army is less vulnerable to the enemy and more visible to everyone else. As any tourist can testify, the Swiss Army is probably the most visible army in the world. In every part of the upper Valais, soldiers are in action.

Each new day adds to the complexity of this multiple-exercise montage. Fusiliers begin to move in co-ordination with machine guns and, before long, with mortars—soldiers on their stomachs under other soldiers' bullets: machine-gun bullets shifting back and

forth from one target to another while advancing fusiliers send bursts from their assault rifles; the two layers
of fire conjoin.

The Swiss make the claim that they do things in
exercises no other army would do. No one disputes the
claim. The Swiss are the sort of people who like to shoot
apples off one another's heads. Bullets fly close. Grenades explode close. Artillery and mortar shells drop
nearby. Flamethrowers throw flames above crawling soldiers. When American troops in training crawl under
machine-gun fire, the barrels of the guns are resting on
metal supports below which they physically cannot
move. Swiss machine guns are set up without constraints,
exactly as in battle. A machine gunner has told me that
he fired twenty-two thousand rounds in a single hour
over the heads of other soldiers. He said the only accident he could remember happened when someone in his
company fired a mortar over a mountain and into the
next valley, where the shell exploded and killed a cow.
In rounds fired—a military statistic of the first importance—the Swiss Army compares favorably with all
other armies. Ammunition is expensive. Use of it begets
skill in the use of it. Rounds fired is a classified matter
everywhere, because analysts use the numbers to assess
preparedness.

One afternoon, the military attachés went into the
Canton de Fribourg to watch hundred-and-six-millimetre
recoilless rifles being fired at targets across a public road.
Automobiles were on the road. In case anyone should
be wondering, it was explained that the drivers were
travelling at their own risk, because notices had been
posted—"AVIS DE TIR"—in the nearest communities to

one side and the other. Machine gunners behind the attachés opened fire over their heads. "I was ready to hit the dirt," one of them said later. "I've been shot at before." A platoon of Swiss riflemen moved forward under the machine-gun fire. Another platoon, off to the right, was contributing rifle fire, too. As the first group moved ever farther forward, the riflemen to the right smoothly adjusted their fire so the bullets would not hit the advancing platoon. All these soldiers were essentially novices, in their fourth week of basic training.

Families sometimes visit units in training and watch them perform exercises. Several months ago, a blank mortar shell bounced off a wall and killed the fiancée of a soldier. Artillery shells, lost in high ground, have been fatal to hikers. Now and again, soldiers die in accidents in army vehicles, and not long ago a soldier fell off a rope bridge and drowned in a river. A woman in Geneva once told me that a friend of her family had lost three fingers to a grenade, and she added bitterly, "It seems so unnecessary when he's never going to have to fight a war."

Her husband lowered his fork. He said, "You hope he's never going to have to fight a war."

Under the Schwarzbergalp, above the Mattmarksee, machine guns, grenades, and rifles in concert open fire. The soldiers seem a little absurd, wearing brown-black-green-and-red camouflage capes in two feet of October snow. In winter, they wear white. The enemy approaches. They respond by throwing snowballs. It is a way of indicating to others where they mean to throw grenades. Now a smoke puff the shape and color of an eggplant comes up from a grenade—and another, and another—while echoes crash on the Schwarzbergalp and avalanches drop like veils.

Machine guns blaze in the Lengtal, four hundred metres above Lax. A helicopter touches down, carrying the Divisionnaire, a councillor of state of the Canton de Vaud, and other itinerant observers. The pilot is asked to move. He has landed on the target. He hops to safer ground—near a tall freestanding white cross, beside the church of the village of Heiligkreuz. Over the ridge, in the Rappetal, rifles, bazookas, and grenades are filling a ravine with smoke and splintered steel. The soldiers are tired, having climbed at night into this cold valley. Arriving before dawn, they slept a few hours on the ground —a student, a butcher, a gardener, an electrician, two farmers. Routinely, soldiers will walk all night in hard rain in order to reach the mountain setting from which they will attack. After arriving, they wash, shave. They prepare and eat hot food. They clean and oil their rifles. Still sleepless, they go into action—in logical formation, with eight to ten yards separating each man from the next. Unskilled soldiers will advance in bunches, congealed by herd instinct. Fire one shot at them and they all spread out—like the Swiss, who lack war experience but are well trained.

On a high slope of the Mattertal, three thousand feet above the valley floor, the noonday sun is shining, and the air is still and warm. Small barns, roofed with slabs of slate, go down to the river like stepping stones. From under a camouflage net, a carpenter fires a mortar vaguely toward the Matterhorn. The Matterhorn appears to be a railroad spike driven through the earth from the other side, or, with its canted summit, the beckoning finger of God. The helicopter ignores the Matterhorn, and, climbing a higher mountain, rises up the face of the Weisshorn. It climbs the rock a grain at a time. It hangs like a lamp before the wall of granite gneiss—Weisshorn: fourteen thousand seven hundred and eighty-two feet—and then floats across the summit ridge into the Val d'Anniviers.

Major Jaussi is there, at eight thousand feet, with his machine guns firing. The guns are shifting rapidly from target to target, firing their tracers into rock. "We have old machine guns," Jaussi remarks. "But in the mountains you need strong material. And these are very precise." They weigh seventeen kilograms. Their tripods weigh sixteen kilograms. Their ammunition (six hundred rounds for each gun) weighs twenty-seven kilograms. All this has been carried up here on the shoulders of the crews. The guns fire in three-second bursts—fifty bullets a burst. Major Jaussi inserts his words between bullets. "The enemy has been discovered," he says. "We want to make surprise fire. Therefore, the two machine guns must open fire together." Automatic rifles join in. Bullets rain into a north-facing cirque across a stream called the Torrent du Marais.

On even higher ground across the valley—the top of a five-hour climb—soldiers are advancing beside an avenue of machine-gun fire into a cirque that is rouged with alpenglow. In two feet of snow, eight soldiers, two with bazookas, cross a rise, fall prone, open fire.

An atomic bomb has exploded in Zweisimmen. The ubiquitous Major Jaussi is now in a village basement, in a house he is using for a command post, deep in the valley. He has received orders to move his battalion to

La Place de la Concorde Suisse

Château-d'Oex, using only mountain routes, for all movement by road is impossible. Overnight and into tomorrow, he and his captains and lieutenants have to figure out how to do it, and get the battalion started, and plan an attack from Gstaad. Captain Ernst Sturzenegger sits beside him. Words are sharp, formal, intensely serious. It is an exercise of the brain of the battalion. The battalion's A.B.C. man—atomic, biological, chemical expert—has already calculated the fallout and what routes to follow. "This is a test of the leaders in a stress situation, close to the real thing," Jaussi explains. Around the building are coils of barbed wire. There are wooden barricades. Airport-size searchlights, at eye level, periodically come on and sweep the night, sweep from house to house in the village. In the clips of the sentries' rifles, the bullets are no less real than they are in the mountains.

A hundred kilometres to the northeast, red helicopters have landed on the Rigi, bringing troops to join a battle in the valley below. On any given day, there is a battle almost anywhere, for "Switzerland does not have an army, Switzerland is an army," as the Swiss are wont to say. The enemy main force is coming down from Lake Constance and is using gas. The Rigi and the Rossberg are subalpine mountains that flank the Valley of Arth and Goldau, south of the Zuger See—in Schwyz, the forest canton for which the Confederation was named. Red tanks are moving south into the valley against established Swiss positions, while red infantry moves along the slopes of the two mountains to close in on the Swiss in pincer attack with the tanks.

The Swiss force is a Landwehr brigade—men in the thirty-three-to-forty-two age group, by dint of time no longer élite. Landwehr brigades are not mobile, like the élite troops. Landwehr brigades do their refresher training in the place they would defend in war. The exact territory of a Landwehr brigade is classified, but for Infantry Battalion 188 it is more or less this valley. In a deep fog, the soldiers are dug in and fighting. Many are in foxholes, with fresh dirt piled beside them. Spread out in ones and twos, they cannot see from foxhole to foxhole. Visibility is less than a hundred feet. The fog is cut only by the throat-clearing sounds of automatic rifles, of machine guns ripping like surgical tape. A man in a gas mask is dug in beside a road in Oberarth. He is under a camouflage net, and he wears a camouflage cape. Intently, he watches the road, all but a bit of it obscure. He has an assault rifle in his hands, and when the enemy tanks come into view he will use it to fire anti-tank grenades. He has waited long, and no tanks have appeared. A man on a bicycle emerges suddenly from the fog—a civilian, middle-aged, with a pipe in his mouth. He rides by, does not seem to notice the soldier, and disappears quickly back into the fog. Across the road is an orchard, and each tree—apple, cherry—is more distinct than the one behind it, evanescing in the fog. Close behind the foxhole, two cows appear, clinking. In their curiosity, they extend their heads under the camouflage net and on either side of the soldier. All three watch the road.

The fog suddenly lifts, all in a moment, as if a light had been switched on in a room. There are sidewalks, houses, apartment buildings, light industry, a school. A Gulf gasoline station is just up the road. There are people on the sidewalks, people on bicycles, a woman behind a baby carriage. The battle is waging not in some remote alpine cirque but in the precincts of a populous town.

Now there is more rifle fire, machine-gun fire. No one so much as looks up. Conversations on the sidewalks do not even pause. The sound might as well be the sound of rumbling trucks. In this community, battlefield noise is just background noise—routine, possibly reassuring. Citizen army at work. Everyone knows the ammunition is blank.

The fog has dropped again, as rapidly as it lifted. The soldier in the gas mask is an electrician, and he wonders if I am legitimate. I am accompanied by Lieutenant Siegward Strub, a friend from Basel, who arranged for me to be here. The soldier turns upon him the flat-glass stare of the gas mask. Strub's uniform notwithstanding, the soldier seems to be wondering if Strub is a lieutenant. The soldier demands identification. Strub gets out his wallet, offers his papers, and makes a note to commend the soldier. To see a Landwehr brigade—and, incidentally, a German-speaking battalion—I have taken a day off from the high mountains and journeyed into the fog. The battle can be followed by ear—by listening to the artillery and the mortars, by listening to the machine guns and the rifles, and, most of all, by listening to Strub. He grew up in Goldau, a mile up the road, and now, in effect, has returned with the brigade to defend his home. Walking through the orchard, we come upon machine-gun nests equipped with anti-aircraft tripods—the better to bring down helicopters. The fog is now so deep the guns could not bring down an apple. The men—two in a nest—are under camouflage nets and are wrapped in camouflage capes as they lie beside their machine guns. They look middle-aged, thin on top, well fed. They have periscope binoculars and infrared sights. Somewhere out there in the fog, red infantry is creeping in, hoping to surprise them. The machine gunners, quietly talking, do not appear to be nervous.

"It's in the air," one of them says. "Something will happen soon."

"What is in the air?" says the other.

"Fog."

For the moment, cowbells in the orchard are the only sound. There is an occasional burst from an automatic rifle. The machine gunners have been in the nests most of the night and day. They take turns going off to a stable to sleep in sleeping bags on straw.

Moving on under the branches of plums, walnuts, and pears, Lieutenant Strub and I soon see in the mist the tall marching columns of the Autobahn to Saint Gotthard crossing a crease in the side of the Rigi. We can scarcely see the outline of the roadway. We hear only the wave-lap swish of the cars as they pass overhead. The road is a four-lane highway to the most strategic Swiss alpine pass, and so it is not surprising that in one of the support columns is a pair of metal doors. Strub looks questioningly at me, and I tell him I know what they are. He says that the miners (the demolitionists) are back in the fog somewhere: in houses, or out-of-doors under nets —in any case, well hidden, he has no idea where. He says the miners are the most secretive people in the army, and when he is having a beer with them and casually asks questions they have no answer for two out of three. For example, he has asked how many metres of this bridge would fall into the orchard if the reds were on their way to the pass. No answer. In their hideouts, meanwhile, the miners have nothing much to do, so they shuffle a deck and play Jass. It is a game with partners and trumps and what have you—a sort of bridge demolishers' bridge. Strub says, "It helps kill time efficiently." Who but the Swiss would have such a talent?

"We say in Switzerland, 'In every country, there is an army; here it is better to have our army than another one,'" Strub remarks, offering his endorsement of the military enterprise. He is a slender man in his thirties with bright brown eyes, a dark mustache, and thick prematurely gray hair that rises straight from his forehead before yielding to gravity and tumbling to the rear. His father was a railway engineer, operating the precision instruments that in other countries are known as trains. Sigi—as Lieutenant Strub is called—went to the University of Zurich and developed an interest in classical genetics. He found that virtually every important paper in the field had been written in English. Translations by and large did not exist. So he began reading English— novels, newspapers. For the better part of four years, he avoided his native German and every other language but English. When he presented his doctoral dissertation to the faculty in Zurich, the dissertation was in English. It was called "Developmental Potentials of Male Fore-Leg Imaginal Disks of Drosophila Melanogaster," and on the strength of it he won a postdoctoral fellowship at the University of California, Irvine. Later, he taught at the State University of New York at Stony Brook, Long Island. Now he is licensing manager for the pharmaceutical division of Sandoz, in Basel. He likens the Landwehr to a net, always in place. "I know exactly where, if the Russians come, I will fight. In this battalion are country people. With them, there is an x and a y axis and maybe a z axis, and that's it. If I had to face a war, I would like it to be with these people. If a lieutenant went ahead, they would follow. We come from this canton and are integrated into the general society here —more, sometimes, than we like, for the supply of schnapps is so constant. In Basel, we drink coffee with kirsch in it. Here we drink kirsch with coffee in it."

The fog is away again, and now we can see not only the Autobahn over the orchard but also the passenger trains on the side of the Rigi, going to or coming from Saint Gotthard. They slide by in comparative silence. They run on falling water. There is a tunnel. Soldiers are ready with bazookas, grenades, and automatic rifles to hit anything that happens to come through it. Machine guns and rifles are firing in the orchard. When machine guns erupt, the tempo of the cowbells does not increase. A woman with a small child drives among the trees in a station wagon. Bazookas are trained on the road, ready for the tanks. If little Haflingers appear, they are meant to be Schützenpanzers—eleven-and-a-half-ton tanks that can go sixty-five kilometres an hour carrying a twenty-millimetre cannon and seven grenadiers. If Pinzgauers appear, they are meant to be heavy tanks. If Fiats appear, they had best be ignored.

Again, the fog drops heavily. After Mark Twain was on the Rigi, in 1878, he wrote, "The fog lifted and showed us a well-worn path which led up a very steep rise to the left. We took it, and as soon as we had got far enough from the railway to render the finding it again an impossibility, the fog shut down on us once more." Fog favors the attacking side. The guns become relatively quiet—an occasional pop . . . pop . . . pop. While

Strub goes off to perform as a referee, I climb a knoll and pass the time with Major Othmar Huber, who hands me his card. Honeywell, Zurich. Like Strub, he grew up here. He once led artillery units, and is now in charge of infantry munitions. The fog has become so thick I cannot see thirty feet beyond him. We are alone on this knoll, like deserted sailors on an island. "We prepare for something well and hope it never happens," he is saying. "We think it necessary. When a Lebanon, a Falklands, an Afghanistan occurs, we analyze each. We try to transform the experience to our purposes."

The fluctuating fog is in recession again, and Strub and other officers are talking in a circle by the school. Close to them, a soldier lies prone on the ground. He has cut some branches from a bush and arranged them over his bazooka. The situation makes him smile. His name is Urs Märchy, and he is a salesman for Sulzer Brothers, Zurich. Two young boys walk by, glance at him without comment or apparent interest—a man with a bazooka lying on the ground outside their school. An old man with a walking stick pays even less attention. The machine gunners we talked with in the orchard are now officially dead. Red infantry surprised them from behind. Their lieutenant died with them. In Strub's unit, half the men are gone. The others are regrouping, blaming the fog. While the officers confer, I stand a little apart, rapidly writing notes. Between my nose and my notepad, there suddenly appears the muzzle of a Sturmgewehr. I look up into the unsmiling eyes of a soldier.

"Sigi! Sigi!"

Strub sees what is happening, comes over, and explains. Leo Fässler, foreman in a factory on the Greifensee, lowers the gun.

It is five hours after midnight, and in absolute darkness the Section de Renseignements sleeps—a deep agglomerate sleep, without a stir. The door opens at one end of the room. Light falls on the nearer bunks. A corporal with a bullhorn voice calls out, "Messieurs, bonjour!"

Reveille is not known by that name here. Here it is called la diane. Call it what you will, the response is complete silence.

Ten minutes later, the corporal tries again. In the continuing silence, Massy alone concedes that he is conscious. Staring upward into the black, he says, "Il fait beau."

Minutes later, the corporal reappears in the doorway and sternly orders everyone up. When the corporal is gone, Massy remarks, "He is thinking that he is a general."

No one else has complained, moaned, stretched, turned over, lifted his head, sat up—or, in fact, moved. When Lieutenant Wyssa arrives, he says exactly nothing, and they begin to stir. They dress, fill their packs. They breakfast on bread and fruit confections. They receive their assignments, calculate itineraries, and prepare for an arduous day. The enemy is everywhere—threatening passes, threatening the hanging valleys, threatening the riparian landscapes of the Rhone. A command post has been established in a small garage in a private home. In addition to the usual note-taking and sketchmaking and assessments of bridges and barns, the patrol today will carry a transceiver and report to the command post coded descriptions of activity in the Valais.

The sky is heavy, but there is brightness at the southern edge. With their packs and assault rifles, the patrol sets out. Walking downhill—among cattle and barns and apple trees in fruit—Jean-Bruno Wettstein tells me that during my absence the Section de Renseignements was visited by Divisionnaire Tschumy. "He said he believed that Switzerland must be defended from the borders by the army. He said a lot of young people, basing their views on Che Guevara and the French Maquis, think guerrilla warfare is the answer, but actually to depend from the outset on guerrilla warfare is to permit your cities to be occupied, and therefore to capitulate. He said, 'We don't want to be occupied. The army must be prepared to meet an invader head-on, because guerrilla warfare is particularly hard on civilians.' The Swiss remember Oradour, the French village that was almost totally murdered—and many similar examples. I believe Tschumy is right. Tschumy is realistic. The Maquis may have been somewhat effective, but their country was already occupied."

A light rain begins to fall. Taking shelter under the

tall concrete pillars of the elevated Simplon road, the soldiers put on rain gear, and turn on the transceiver to send their first coded message: "THE REDS ARE USING POISON GAS AT GRIMSELPASS."

The code consists of three-digit numbers, which represent phrases that are recorded in a top-secret book. An infantry battalion, for example, is a 200. A message might read, "200 206 195 495 202 322 999." One does not easily learn to compose such tight prose, and in the Section de Renseignements there is particular need for practice.

"ROUGE A PARACHUTÉ SUR GRIMSELPASS."

"We are Boy Scouts," Wettstein comments as the message goes out.

They are, at any rate, four today—Massy, Wettstein, Pillard, and Pierre Gabus, a Geneva lawyer. They are descending into Brig—Roman Brig, staging point for travellers preparing to cross the Simplon, a historically imbricate town. To walk to its center from the outside is to go from basketball courts and light industry into neighborhoods of the nineteenth and eighteenth centuries and on into Renaissance vestiges and cobblestoned medieval streets. In the covered Metzgergasse, the soldiers step out of the rain and transmit another message: "RED ARTILLERY IS HITTING THE NUFENENPASS."

They have leaned their rifles against the window of a textile shop, in front of a display of cotton sweatshirts, on one of which is lettered "U.S. BASEBALL NEW YORK."

"U.S. cultural infiltration," Wettstein remarks. "That is a typical Swiss shirt."

It is true. In all parts of Switzerland, people wear shirts that say "CALIFORNIA UNIVERSITY" or "FLORIDA UNIVERSITY" or "NEW YORK UNIVERSITY." One afternoon among the walking rich on the Bahnhofstrasse in Zurich, I saw a tall young woman roasting and selling chestnuts, her ocean-swell breasts filling a Harvard sweatshirt.

The rain stops. The patrol moves on, and passes a Bridge of Sighs connecting two parts of a seventeenth-century palace. Wettstein says, "Now forget the army for a minute and look at that."

In Sebastiansplatz, everyone stops to drink at the fountain commemorating George Chávez, the first man to fly out of Switzerland and cross the Alps in an airplane. He crashed and died on the other side.

On the Bahnhofstrasse of Brig are many shoppers, none of whom shows any surprise on seeing a patrol of soldiers with assault rifles coming down the street, just as the citizens of Oberarth were not surprised to find a battle taking place in their town. Massy's attention is arrested by a Prontophot booth in the foyer of a Jelmoli store opposite the Walliser Kantonalbank. For a coin or two, the booth will produce a passport-size photograph. The soldiers stack their rifles against a table of dry flowers, for sale in bunches, two francs a bunch. All five of us, stacked one on another, under Massy's direction assemble in the booth. We freeze before the lens. While we wait for the picture, a message goes out, Prontophot booth to command post, now hear this: "ONE COMPANY OF MOTORIZED ENEMY FUSILIERS HAS LANDED IN HELICOPTERS BETWEEN MÜNSTER AND THE RHONE. AN ENEMY SECTION DE RENSEIGNEMENTS HAS CROSSED THE NIEDERWALD." It appears that we have a red rival.

Having traversed the city, the patrol reaches the Rhone—here a green running river with frequent patches of white. There are two bridges not far apart. Massy sketches them and records data on their structures and dimensions. The soldiers cross the river, walk downstream along the right bank, and stop to admire a big steel bucket that slides several hundred metres down a cable, splashes into the rapids, picks up a few tons of gravel, and emerges from the river to ascend to a cement plant. After the big steel bucket has made six round trips, they turn and face the Bernese Oberland. It begins only a few feet away, as the terrain rises sharply from the river.

According to instructions, the patrol is to climb some distance and check out possibilities. The first possibility is that we will fall off the cliffside into the Rhone. The climb is efficient, in the sense that almost every step is up. Where the going is particularly steep, there are cables to hang on to—put here, says Massy, by farmers. It is a trail of short switchbacks, now among scattered trees, now across rock face. Astonishingly soon, the view expands. The Rhone seems a long plunge below. In Brig, over the river, we can see the green where the battalion held its Prise du Drapeau, the marble yard, the Saltina coming down from Simplon, the twin dark holes of the railway tunnels to Italy. In the long perspective to the west, the walls of the Rhone Valley seem to come together and close. In the middle ground is the jet strip at Turtmann. Massy is reciting numbers into the walkie-talkie: "A COMPANY OF SWISS FUSILIERS IS WITH DIFFI-CULTY HOLDING TURTMANN." The sun comes and goes in a sky of breaking cloud.

In all, we climb about fourteen hundred feet before the terrain leans back—as a pronouncedly inclined alpage. The view is now panoptic—over the deep-set river to the white summits, the long front line of the

Pennines leading the eye west. Twenty miles down-stream, the valley bends slightly and cuts the view. Above the river, avalanche tracks stripe the mountain-sides between dark gorges no machine could pass. The floor of the valley is groomed and industrial. There are rows of Lombardy poplars along airstrips that serve no city. This centerland of the Valais, with its vegetable fields and orchards, too—its apples and asparagus, to-matoes and pears—would appear to be an ultimate citadel for the democracy, where the nation could attempt an impregnable stand. As if the mountains were not barrier enough, ancient landslides have left their natural barri-cades at intervals down the valley.

A farmhouse near the alpage is checked out for water and habitation. There is enough of both for one company. We make our way on upward and—with some surprise, as always—climb onto a curving moun-tain road.

"A COMPANY OF FUSILIERS HAS PARACHUTED INTO THE NUFENENPASS."

We walk west about a kilometre, with the Pennine Alps to our left, the Rhone deep below, and come into a vertical village, stacked up facing the sun. There is a restaurant called Restaurant. Inside is a long table by a window looking at the mountains. In the restaurant's umbrella stand the patrol stands four assault rifles. Half-litre glasses of beer are soon on the table by the window. The prospect is giddy—a long fall down the mountain-side and deep into le trou. I remember Lieutenant Strub saying, "Basically, with age, you become sly in the army, and you know in which restaurant you will find the soldiers, and the slyness is a military advantage if an enemy comes."

La Place de la Concorde Suisse

The walkie-talkie is set up on the table, its antenna inclining toward the light. Massy strings numbers with a pencil on a pad. He reports to the command post, "A COMPANY OF MOTORIZED RED FUSILIERS HAS DESCENDED FROM THE NUFENENPASS AND HAS REACHED ULRICHEN."

From Birgisch, as this village is called, the patrol is to return with an aerial sketch of the valley environs of Brig. Pierre Gabus looks out the window and draws one, deftly.

Fondue arrives—authoritative with kirsch and bubbling with the Fendant of Valais. An alcohol flame spreads flat on the bottom of the pot, browning the edges of the cheese inside. There is a transition from beer to wine. Massy pours. Wettstein says, "The army needs marginal people. They know that in an emergency if there's a job to be done we'll do it. That's why they leave us alone. We agree to walk and to shoot, but for us it is difficult to submit to discipline."

Long forks are flying. The fondue is surpassingly good. Four new customers have taken seats at a nearby table. They see the situation and are obviously amused. They are men, dressed in wool shirts, and are stopping in from work—farmers probably, at any rate civilians, but, of course, they are also in the army. They laugh. They jeer. They exhibit a mixture of mockery and empathy. When Massy lifts the transceiver and reads off a set of numbers, they moo in unison, helping the command post to imagine a bucolic scene.

"Moooo."

"LA GARE DE BRIGUE A ÉTÉ DÉTRUITE PAR LES SABOTEURS."

"Moooo."

"A BATTALION OF ENEMY MOTORIZED FUSILIERS HAS

LANDED IN HELICOPTERS IN THE PLAIN OF THE RHONE BE-
TWEEN TURTMANN AND THE RIVER."

"Compris! Compris! Moooo."

Massy holds the transceiver even higher, turns it
upside down, and stirs the fondue with the antenna. He
wipes it off and calls in another message: "A PEASANT
IN OBERWALD HAS SEEN FOUR ARMORED CARS COMING OUT
OF ST. NIKLAUS AND HEADING FOR THE VALLEY."

As the alcohol burns on, the golden crust is ever
more delicious, scraped from the edge of the fondue.
Dessert is coupe Danemark—four and a half francs'
worth of whipped cream over ice cream under ductile
chocolate. There are five wee glasses of kirsch.

Wettstein waxes declarative, saying, "This is the
best day I have spent in the Swiss Army."

On winter marches in the time of the Borgias, it was
thought that Swiss soldiers, in their cold armor, might
lose too much body heat. Accordingly, they were given
orders never to drink water but to quench all thirst with
schnapps.

"TWO COMPANIES OF ENEMY MOTORIZED FUSILIERS
HAVE REACHED RARON. ABOUT FIFTEEN ARMORED VEHICLES
HAVE BEEN DESTROYED."

Massy signals for a check and knocks back the last
of the kirsch. Again he lifts the transceiver. There is
more to report before we go.

"AN ATOMIC BOMB OF PETITE SIZE HAS BEEN DROPPED
ON SIERRE. OUR BARRICADES AT VISP STILL HOLD. THE
BRIDGES OF GRENGIOLS ARE SECURE. WE ARE IN CONTACT
WITH THE ENEMY."

M EMORIES OF S UMMER

Also by Ruth White

S W E E T   C R E E K   H O L L E R

W E E P I N G   W I L L O W

B E L L E   P R A T E R ' S   B O Y

J
W

Memories of Summer

Ruth White

OLD CHARLES TOWN LIBRARY, INC.
200 E. WASHINGTON ST.
CHARLES TOWN, WV 25414

FARRAR STRAUS GIROUX ❦ NEW YORK

0003075

Copyright © 2000 by Ruth White
All rights reserved
Distributed in Canada by Douglas & McIntyre Ltd.
Printed in the United States of America
Designed by Filomena Tuosto
First edition, 2000
10 9 8 7 6 5 4 3 2 1

Excerpt from *The Little Prince* by Antoine de Saint-Exupéry, copyright ©
1943 and renewed © 1971 by Harcourt, Inc., reprinted by permission of the
publisher.

Lyric excerpts of "Sisters" by Irving Berlin (pages 10 and 65), copyright ©
1953 by Irving Berlin, copyright renewed. International copyright secured. All
rights reserved. Reprinted by permission.

Lyrics from "Moments to Remember": music by Robert Allen; lyrics by Al
Stillman; copyright © 1955, renewed and assigned to Larry Spier, Inc., New
York, and to Charlie Dietcher Productions, Inc., Quogue, New York.
Reprinted by permission.

Library of Congress Cataloging-in-Publication Data
White, Ruth, date.
    Memories of Summer / Ruth White.— 1st ed.
        p.   cm.
    Summary: In 1955, thirteen-year-old Lyric finds her whole life changing
when her family moves from the hills of Virginia to a town in Michigan and
her older sister Summer begins descending into mental illness.
    ISBN 0-374-34945-2
        [1. Mentally ill—Fiction.   2. Sisters—Fiction. 3. Michigan—Fiction.
4. Mountain life—Virginia—Fiction. 5. Virginia—Fiction.   6. Moving,
Household—Fiction.] I. Title.
    PZ7.W58446 Me   2000
    [Fic]—dc21   99-54793

dedicated to
the memory of my sister, Audrey

If someone loves a flower, of which just one single
blossom grows in all the millions and millions of stars,
it is enough to make him happy just to look at the stars.
He can say to himself,
"Somewhere, my little flower is there . . ."

—*The Little Prince* by Antoine de Saint-Exupéry

MEMORIES OF SUMMER

one

My parents knew no other place but the southwest Virginia hills where they were raised. I didn't remember Mama, because she died of consumption when I was three and my sister was six. But relatives told us she had been a gentle person who read poetry and the Bible, and sang hymns beautifully.

We affectionately called our daddy Poppy, and many times he related to us what Mama had decided long before we were born.

"Our children will have no common names," she had said to him. "A name should have meaning, and tell other folks something about the person. It should help you find your place in this life, and make you feel like you're worth something."

So when my older sister was born, Mama had said, "We'll call this one Summer, and she'll grow up just a'sparklin' with warmth and laughter, and the world will be a brighter place with her in it."

And when I was born, Mama had said, "We'll call this

one Lyric, and she'll be a singer of songs so sweet it'll bring tears to your eyes."

Poppy spent a year watching Mama waste away to nothing before she finally died, and he always said it was the sorriest year of his life, not just because he lost her, but on top of that, his daddy, our Grandpa Compton, died in a mining accident. Poppy told us he hoped and prayed his girls would never have to suffer through a time like that.

Everybody in Glory Bottom knew Grandpa. When the explosion boomed, Grandpa and six other men were trapped in this little bitty space, cut off from the rest of the mine, sealed in tight as a tomb. The foreman, who had been away to the college and knew about such things, calculated how long they could survive in this small area cramped with seven bodies breathing. And what he said was if they were still and didn't exert too much energy, and didn't breathe any more than was necessary, they had maybe an hour to live. So they sat quiet and waited and prayed for deliverance before the hour was up.

Grandpa was the only one wearing a watch, and ever so often he would hold it up to the carbide lamp on his miner's helmet and softly call out the time to the trapped men. The others thought it was peculiar for him to do such a thing, but they didn't mention it, maybe 'cause they were curious to know how much time they had left on this earth. But the most peculiar thing of all was when the rescuers finally got there, Grandpa was the only dead man amongst them. Somebody figured out they had been trapped almost two hours instead of one. Grandpa had called out the wrong time, making the men think they had more time than they did, just so they wouldn't give up hope. But he was wearing the watch, so only he knew the truth!

Poppy had always been a good ole boy, just happy to be a coal miner like his daddy and his daddy's daddy. But he changed after Mama and Grandpa died. Where he usta go out gambling and carousing, and spending his money on liquor, now he stayed home, and took up reading the Bible and going to church with us.

Poppy also had the reputation of being the best guitar picker this side of Nashville. He could play any tune you could hum, and he was always saying that it was his mission in life to give joy, to make people sing and dance and laugh.

So it was just as Mama had predicted—in spite of our loss of her, me and Summer grew up singing and laughing. Poppy was always there like a rock, and we felt safe and loved. Our childhood was happy.

But it was Summer I remember bathing me and kissing away the bumps and bruises. Summer patty-caking and rockabye-babying. Reading to me. Summer packing my lunch and taking me to my first day of school. Leading me by the hand to the outhouse in the morning dew. Holding my forehead when I threw up. Plaiting my hair. Hushing me in Sunday School.

We roamed the hills and creeks, picking daisies and tiger lilies, black-eyed Susans, Indian paintbrushes, and wild pink roses. We slid downhill on golden leaves. We climbed trees and explored caves, and peeped into abandoned mines. But we didn't go in there. They were scary. We dammed up the creek and made swimmin' holes. But best of all, we told each other our secrets and dreams.

Poppy had never owned a car. He didn't even know how to drive, so we walked everywhere we went. If it was too far to walk, there was a bus that went to some places. If we couldn't get there by bus, we had to find somebody with a car to take us. If we couldn't do that, we stayed home. And that's what we did most of the time. Stayed home.

We liked each other and we entertained each other. We read books and played games. We listened to the radio. We made fudge and went to quiltings, to school and church and to the picture show at the county seat. We saw relatives at Thanksgiving and Decoration Day.

Me and Summer learned to cook pretty good. Poppy helped us raise a garden, and we canned things for cold weather. We bought our clothes cheap at the company store or from a mail-order catalog. So we had everything we needed. Then why did we dream about going somewheres else and making more money and having more stuff? It's a mystery. I don't know why, but it was a continuing thread that pulled the years together. Someday we will leave this place. Someday we will have a white house. Someday we will have more money and buy things.

Poppy taught me and Summer to harmonize, and we got real good at it. Everybody said so. Summer's voice was high and clear like a bell, while mine was low and mellow like a clarinet. And people were always asking us to sing for them. We could be going down the road to the store, or coming home from the show, and somebody was liable to step out on their porch and holler, "Come on in here, girls, and sing us a song!" So we did. And they paid us nickels and dimes, sometimes quarters, depending on who it was.

We sang for fun even when we didn't get paid, simply because we loved it. Lots of times we sung places with Poppy—parties and church gatherings mostly. But any place there was an audience, they might ask us to pick and sing. I reckon we were famous in our neck of the woods.

Summer always did have funny ways about her, but I got so used to them, they seemed normal to me. For example, she was scared to death of electricity. Poppy called it a "terror" and he said it started when Summer was a baby and stuck her finger in a live socket. But Summer said she didn't even remember that, and she thought it started when she stepped on an electric cord that was frayed. Both times she was shocked.

But whenever it happened, her fear of electricity kept her from doing some ordinary things. Like pulling the cord to turn on the light in a dark room. Me or Poppy had to do that for her. She wouldn't even turn on the radio. We had to do that for her too, and then adjust the static out of it. We also had a fan that she wouldn't touch. In fact, she would pull her dress tail aside to keep from brushing it when she passed by. But the Frigidaire was something else. She wasn't a bit afraid of it. She said it was because it was cold. So it didn't seem to be electric. She thought of electricity as hot. We had nothing else that was electric, except lights on our Christmas tree once a year.

Another odd thing was Summer's fear of dogs. She would panic and hide whenever she saw one. She always called them wolves. She'd say she heard a wolf barking, or a wolf wanted to bite her, when it was really just a little doggie trying to play.

I liked dogs myself, and one time Poppy got us a puppy, hoping Summer would get over her terror. But she wouldn't have it in the house. She cried and cried until Poppy gave the puppy away to kinfolks. I didn't fault her for that. She couldn't help how she felt.

She had some other peculiarities too, like rocking her body when she was upset, just rocking and moaning. Or shaking her leg. That would drive her teachers nuts, and they would always put her in the back row, so they wouldn't see that leg going to town.

And Summer talked to herself. People would laugh at her when they caught her doing it, especially the other kids. And she would turn real red in the face. She told me secretly that beings appeared to her that nobody else could see, and that's who she was talking to.

I got mad at folks when they laughed at Summer, but as she got older she started whispering to the invisible ones, instead of talking out loud, so others were not as apt to notice. She was always looking up toward the hills, listening and whispering. And I didn't think Summer strange at all, because she was my sister and I had grown up with her whispering to the hills.

two

August 9, 1955, Summer's sixteenth birthday, was a hot day, relieved by a gentle afternoon shower, so that the deep holler where we lived between the mountains lay cool in shadows. It smelled of rain and earth.

We were on the front porch. Summer's friends Jewel and Ethel were there, as well as Anderson Biddle. He was a town boy, and that's why we called him by his whole and complete name. You did that with town folks.

I remember the sky was pink late that evening and Jewel said it meant that somebody was going to die.

" 'Course somebody's gonna die," Summer said. "Somebody dies every day!"

I had turned thirteen in March, and I could bake cakes pretty good. I baked one for Summer, and it was white with sixteen yellow candles on it. I remember how Summer's blue eyes sparkled. She looked so pretty that day.

"I wish . . . I wish . . . I wish for a black horse and a silver saddle!" she said with a giggle, and blew out the candles quick.

"Now it won't come true!" I protested. "You told!"

She slipped a butcher knife into the cake with a soft ker-plump! And when she pulled it out, there was icing curled around the sharp edges.

"It won't come true anyways," she said. "That's why I always wish for something I don't really want. Then I won't be disappointed, see?"

We had been dancing to the radio throughout the evening, and me and Summer put our arms around each other and harmonized on a song just the way Rosemary Clooney and Vera Ellen did it in a movie called *White Christmas*.

> *Sisters, sisters,*
> *There were never such devoted sisters . . .*

We had to sit through that movie four times before we got all the words right.

> *All kinds of weather, we stick together,*
> *The same in the rain and sun.*
> *Two diff'rent faces, but in tight places*
> *We think and we act as one.*
> *Uh-huh!*

That last part was especially true. One time me and Summer even dreamed the same dream. We both woke up the next morning babbling about wearing a red dress, and flying over the river. Another thing we did ever once in a while was to bust out singing the same song at the same time! It was uncanny.

There were more words to "Sisters," and we sang it all.

Our audience laughed and clapped. Summer finished cutting the cake and everybody reached for a piece. Poppy came out and sat in a rocking chair, slightly apart from us, smoking his pipe. I handed him some cake on a saucer.

We had Kool-Aid in jelly glasses, and Anderson Biddle said, "Whoo . . . ee!" as he sipped some with his face all screwed up. "It's sour enough to make a pig squeal!"

He was right. It *was* a bit short on the sugar.

"Here's my present, Summer," I said as I placed it, wrapped in soft white tissue paper, on the table that held the cake and stuff.

"Lyric! You shouldn't a'done that!" she said, but I could tell she was pleased.

It was only Precious Pink nail polish. But Summer acted like it was the crown jewels. She always tried to make me feel good like that.

Anderson Biddle gave her a great big bottle of Evening in Paris, and Ethel and Jewel, her *so-called* friends, didn't give her anything. When we were quiet again, everybody looked toward Poppy. We were wondering what he had got for his oldest girl on her sixteenth birthday. For a few days now he had been acting like the cat that swallowed the canary.

"I don't have a proper wrapped-up gift, Summer," he said. "Just some good news."

Summer pushed brown hair out of her pretty face with sticky fingers and looked at him.

"But it's my gift to you," Poppy went on, trying not to smile. "I saved it 'specially for your birthday."

"News 'bout what?"

We looked at Poppy, quiet and waiting.

For a moment even the frogs and crickets quit their evening chatter, and listened for the thing Poppy had to say. Jewel and Ethel and Anderson Biddle stopped eating.

"We're finally moving to Michigan."

"No foolin'?" Summer said breathlessly.

"You got the money?" I said.

"Yeah, I managed to squeeze out the last few dollars we need for bus fare. And Henry wrote me last week. He's found us a place to live. It's even got furniture in it."

Now he was smiling outright.

"All the way to Michigan?" I said in a whisper.

"What's in Michigan?" Anderson Biddle said.

Hadn't he heard all the talk about the car industry in Michigan, how it was booming up there, and anybody could get a job? I guess not.

"We're going to Flint, where they make Chevrolets and Buicks," Summer said. "Poppy's friend Henry went up there and got a job bolting on window cranks. He gets paid good money for that. Poppy's gonna work in a factory, and so am I when I'm old enough."

"No, you're not!" Poppy said emphatically. "My girls are going to school and take up typewriting. A girl can get a good job if she can type."

"I don't want a *good* job," Summer said, emphasizing *good* like it was a dirty word. "I wanna work in the factory."

"My girls are gonna learn typewriting," Poppy said again, even more emphatically.

Summer shrugged. Anderson Biddle was watching her. He was in love with her. They had met in school, and he drove up Glory Bottom two or three times a week to court her. But even though he was a town boy and got to drive his daddy's car places, Summer didn't like him *that* way. She just liked the idea of having somebody in love with her.

"So you're going away?" he said pitifully.

"What day are we leaving on?" Summer said to Poppy, ignoring Anderson Biddle.

"Around the second week in September. First I have to send seventeen dollars up front for the apartment Henry found us."

Apartment? That sounded refined. People in movies lived in apartments. I had never been in one.

"Are you coming back?" Anderson Biddle said.

"I hope not!" Summer spat out the words. "I hate this place!"

"Have you ever lived anywheres else?" Jewel said.

"You know I ain't," Summer said.

Anderson Biddle watched her some more. She was wearing a green sleeveless dress that Poppy had bought her at the company store last spring. The full skirt swirled around her prettily as she twirled around a porch post. Some people said me and Summer looked alike, and it made me so proud.

"Then how do you know you hate this place?" Ethel said crankily. "Michigan might be worse! I betcha never thought of that!"

She was acting ugly. Maybe she was mad because we were leaving and she had to stay here.

A car was snaking up the dirt road. We all stopped talking and looked to see who it was. It was the Ratliffs' car, and we reckoned that was Mr. Ratliff driving, but he was so covered up with coal dust it was hard to say for sure.

"I'm sick to death of the coal mines," Poppy said. "And it's the only living to be made in this place!"

"My daddy don't work in the mines!" Anderson Biddle said with contempt. "He owns half of the A&P!"

He had his nose stuck so far up in the air, a good rain woulda drownded him.

"Well, lah-de-dah," Jewel said. "Which half does he own?"

We all howled then, except for Poppy, and he was trying not to smile.

"Maybe he owns the half where that old clabbered milk is!" Ethel squealed with glee.

"Or the back part there where they got that withered lettuce!" Summer cracked.

Anderson Biddle was not amused.

"You can laugh," he said seriously. "But if you'd stay here, Summer, and marry me like I ast you to, it'd be half yours, too, someday."

I was wondering how many halves were in that store.

But I bit my tongue and didn't say it, 'cause Anderson Biddle had shut us all up. We waited for a response from Summer. A night owl started up. The fireflies were savoring every moment of their brief glory, just flittin' and glowin' in the summer dusk. We could barely see each other's faces. A cool breeze moved through the holler.

"She's too young to marry!" Poppy snapped. "And she's going to Michigan with me and Lyric."

"Yeah, all the way to Michigan," Summer said dreamily, as she gazed at the dark silhouettes of the hills against the sky. The pink glow was all gone by then.

"Just me and Poppy and Lyric, nobody else," she went on. "I'm not going to marry you, Anderson Biddle."

He slapped his glass of Kool-Aid down on the table, and some of it sloshed on me.

"Lookit what you did to my dress, Anderson Biddle!" I hollered at him.

He ignored me, and hissed right in Summer's face, "You'll be sorry!"

Then he left.

Ethel and Jewel giggled.

"Marry him?"

"Yeah, who'd marry him?"

Summer was quiet then. Maybe it was because she was thinking she probably wouldn't get to ride in Anderson Biddle's daddy's car anymore. Or maybe she was just give out from her big day. But I knew it wasn't because she was sorry to lose Anderson Biddle.

Drek'ly the party broke up, and Jewel switched on a flashlight she had with her so she and Ethel could see to walk down the road to their houses. They left, and we figured by this time tomorrow everybody up and down the holler would know the Comptons were moving to Flint, Michigan, come September.

Poppy went in to listen to the news on the radio. Summer stayed on the porch, and I stayed with her, but she was in no talkin' mood.

The Milky Way was shimmering, and the moon came over the mountain, round and silver as a coin. I remember how Summer watched it. Much later, when I went to my bed beside the open window, I could hear her still out there in the moonlight whispering, whispering . . .

I slept long and deep in our little house in the bottom, dreaming of things we would buy in Michigan—like lavender dresses and lace curtains.

three

for the trip we packed only our clothes, Poppy's guitar, and a few other things we couldn't part with. Poppy sold our furniture for practically nothing. Then he picked up his paycheck and we said goodbye to folks. Poppy said he had one more check coming to him, and Oliver Altizer, the clerk there at the mining company, was going to mail it to us.

We had butterflies when we left the bus depot. Shortly we were out of Virginia, and then Kentucky, where we watched the bronze-fringed mountains fall behind us. We rode through Ohio in the chilly September night, laying over in Columbus, where we ate hot dogs wrapped in warm, moist buns, and drank steaming coffee from thick white cups. We stopped in small towns where we made up stories about the people behind the doors, dreaming in their beds, unaware that the Comptons were passing through.

We fell asleep in the farmlands, and woke up with a golden sun spilling over the rim of the world. We had never seen flat land before, much less a real sunrise over a distant horizon. The three of us looked at each other with wide eyes, then back at the spectacle again, wonder-struck.

We reached Flint in mid-morning, and Henry was there to greet us. He carried us in his pickup truck to our apartment on Glenwood Avenue. Such an elegant name for a street! But it was not an elegant place to live, oh, no. We went to the second floor of a house where the Miller family with five small children lived downstairs.

Our "apartment" was a bedroom with two beds and a dresser, no closet, just a rod hung across a corner; then there was a kitchen, wallpapered with grease-splattered barnyard animals, a gas cook stove, the first Frigidaire prob'ly ever made, and a table with four mismatched chairs. Between the two rooms there was a square hallway that had a big old deep sink for washing dishes and clothes, the stairway, and a low window you could crawl out of and walk on the roof if you had a mind to. We had to go downstairs to share the bathroom with the Millers.

Our disappointment showed.

"Well, it's all I could get!" Henry said irritably. "What did y'all expect for seventeen dollars?"

"It's not for long," Poppy said to me and Summer after Henry was gone. "We'll get a bigger and better place soon's I get on at the factory. I promise."

Then he said, "You girls can have the bedroom."

He pulled the littlest bed—actually, it was a cot—into the kitchen for himself to sleep in. Me and Summer sat on the edge of the other bed, quiet for a minute; then we started hanging up our clothes on the rod in the corner.

We knew nothing about Michigan before we got there, except that it was cold, and people talked fancy. For instance, where we said, "No foolin'?" they said, "Really?" Only they didn't pronounce it *rill-y* as we did. They pronounced it *ree-al-lee*, like it had three syllables.

Now we learned some more stuff. Saginaw Street, in downtown Flint, was made out of bricks. We couldn't get over it. We wondered how many bricks it took to do that. And they had traffic lights we didn't know how to use. We stood on the street corners and looked at the lights, and some of them were red and some of them were green and some of them were yellow. We knew you had to stop on red and you could go on green, but what did you do on yellow? Then Henry told us yellow meant go real fast.

But there were lights all above the street, and we didn't know which one we were supposed to look at. It was embarrassing to stand there and watch one string of cars go, then another string, and you didn't know when to go yourself. It made you feel inferior. So we'd turn around and act like we had changed our mind about crossing the street until somebody came along who looked like they knew what they were doing. Then we followed them.

The Flint River ran behind our house, and beyond that was a Chevrolet factory. People just called it Chevrolet.

They'd say, "I work for Chevrolet," or, "That man works for Buick," or, "My brother works for Fisher Body."

That week Poppy went around to the factories putting in his application, or he went off somewhere with Henry, so he said me and Summer could postpone going to school for another week. And he let us run around the city by ourselves and get to know the place. We thought we'd died and gone to heaven. The first thing we did was find the movie theaters. There were so many of them! There was a Rialto, a Capitol, and a Palace. Each theater played a different movie every few days, and they charged you only a quarter to get in. We could walk to them, so we went to a lot of shows. There were buses all over the place, but we were used to walking, and besides, we didn't know which one to take.

Another thing we did that week was go to the Flint Centennial celebrations. The city was one hundred years old that year, and they had a lot of special events going on that week that were all free. Our favorite one was a big to-do in Atwood Stadium. Dinah Shore and her husband, George Montgomery, were there, singing and putting on the dog. We had never seen a celebrity. After the show we stood about ten feet away from Dinah Shore, but we couldn't get any closer. She was talking to some dignitaries, and rubbing Jergens lotion on her hands like an ordinary person.

They had searchlights going back and forth, back and forth across the sky over the city. We learned they were part of the celebrations, and would go on throughout the centennial year.

One evening in the lobby of this big fancy hotel called the Durant, there were tables set up with food like we'd never seen before. You could go in there and get all the free goodies you could eat, and nobody asked you who you were or what you were doing there.

It was the best week of our whole lives, and we ate more, laughed more, celebrated more, and saw more movies than all the other weeks of our life put together.

Every morning we woke up singing, and every night we went to bed humming.

And Summer said, "Do you think it'll always be this way, Lyric?"

Yes, I did.

four

ut the first week ended, and we had to go to school. I joined the eighth-grade class at Zimmerman Junior High School on Corunna Road, but Summer was in the eleventh grade, and she had to go to Central. She also had to ride the city bus, and that scared her. They didn't have school buses in Flint. That was peculiar to us. We thought everybody had school buses. I was close enough to Zimmerman I could walk.

The other students at Zimmerman had been in class since Labor Day, so they were adjusted and I was the new kid.

I changed classes six times and I got lost every one of those six times. I had never changed classes before. I had four men teachers! I had never had a man teacher before. The girls had to take home economics, and the boys shop. Everybody had to take physical education, and I was told I would have to buy a blue gym suit for three dollars, and white sneakers. I already had the shoes, only we called them tennis shoes.

My homeroom teacher assigned me a locker and a combination lock, but I couldn't get it to work. I had to tell a boy my combination so he could open it for me.

When I sat down at a table by myself in the cafeteria to eat my baloney sandwich, I saw that I was the only person who brought their lunch in a poke. The others were eating baked ham with a pineapple ring and a cherry on top of it, which they bought right there in the cafeteria for thirty cents.

Some kids looked at me funny; others acted ugly to me, and a boy named Dewey even called me a name. Then a kind girl named Gladys sat down with me and tried to start a conversation. She told me her daddy was in management at Buick. He caught airplanes out at Willow Run Airport, and flew everywhere. He was gone nearly all the time, she said sadly. I figured I was lucky to have Poppy home with me every night.

I opened my mouth to say something like that, but I was so nervous the words wouldn't come out. Then I couldn't swallow my baloney sandwich, and I had to go to the bathroom to spit it out. I hoped I didn't insult her after she had been nice to me.

It was the worse day of my life, but Summer's day musta been worse than mine. When I got to the apartment I found her already there, curled up like a spring on top of the chenille bedspread. She wouldn't talk to me. Even when I told her my day was bad, too. Even when I asked her if she wanted to walk up to the drugstore on the corner and play the jukebox. Even when I told her supper was on the table. She just laid there and never said a word.

Me and Poppy ate fried potatoes, canned green beans, corn bread, and fruit cocktail for dessert. He asked me about school, and I knew I couldn't make him understand how awful it was, so I told him I'd have to get used to it. Then I told him about the gym suit.

"Tell your teacher you'll have to wait till I get my last pay from the mines," Poppy said.

"But everybody else has theirs already," I said.

"Well, I can't help it," Poppy said. "Tell your teacher what I said. Or I'll write a note. Do you want me to write a note?"

No, I didn't want him to write a note. I wanted the gym suit.

"I'll write a note. And I'll just tell her we don't have the money," Poppy said. "I'll just tell her."

It was clear when Poppy was agitated. He repeated things.

"But they won't let me take P.E. till I get the gym suit. Everybody has to have a gym suit to take P.E.," I said.

Now I was doing it, too.

"Why won't they let you take a pee?" Poppy said.

I had to laugh. And it was good to laugh. It was good to be there with Poppy where I could be the same old me I had always been. I felt better.

"Does Summer have to have a gym suit, too?" Poppy said after I explained P.E. to him.

"I don't know," I said. "Ain't she talked to you?"

"Not a word. I reckon she feels bad. First days are always bad. Tomorrow'll be better."

Poppy was right and he was wrong. School got better for me. But not for Summer.

Even though the teachers at Zimmerman Junior High didn't know my family tree clear back to its roots in England the way the teachers in Virginia did, they treated me like I was a real person anyways. Some of them even made me feel special.

My P.E. teacher smiled and put her arm around me when I gave her Poppy's note. She said it was O.K. to wait for the gym suit, and she said I could be her assistant till I got it. So I started breathing normal again that day.

Yeah, it was the teachers who saved me. But Summer was not saved. She came home the second day and went out on the roof, but there were no hills out there to talk to, only Chevrolet across the river. Finally, she came in and ate supper with us. That day we had navy beans with onions, corn bread, and milk. Poppy said tomorrow we could have pork chops.

"Don't make me go back," Summer pleaded.

"You know you have to go to school," Poppy said.

"Please don't make me," she said again. "I can get a job washing dishes at a restaurant. Henry said I could."

"You have to go to school."

"I'm sixteen. I can quit if I wanna."

"Not so long as I live and breathe."

Somehow we made it through the first week. Gladys became my friend. She was sweet. I told her about coming up from Virginia, about Summer going to Central, and about Poppy trying to get on at General Motors. Gladys introduced me to Nadine. She was a quiet, tall girl from Kentucky. Her daddy worked for Buick too, and she talked just like me.

On Friday night Summer was almost her happy self again, and we went skipping down to Saginaw Street, where they were roping off the traffic for a street dance. We bought cotton candy and strolled around amongst the people, trying to talk fancy, and acting like we had never lived anywhere else.

There was a cute boy who flirted with Summer. She fluttered her eyelids at him, and finally he asked her to dance. Away she went into the street amongst the folks. Old and young alike were dancing together on the brick pavement. I watched Summer and the boy. It was a square dance, and they twirled 'round and 'round under the streetlights, laughing and yelling "Yee-haw!" with everybody else. And I thought she was nearabout the prettiest thing there in her baby-blue dress and crinolines.

Afterwards the boy followed her around, begging for her telephone number. She didn't tell him we had no phone. She gave him an impish grin and tossed her head back. Her face was shining.

"I know you just wanna break my heart, Cutie Pie!" she said to him.

My heart swelled up with pride. That was something Bette Davis might say. Why couldn't I think of feisty things like that to say when a boy talked to me? All I could do was get tongue-tied and red in the face.

We got home late and went to the bathroom. It was right beside the Millers' kitchen. Summer stayed outside the bathroom door while I went in and turned on the light. She watched the Millers and their friends at the kitchen table where they were playing cards and drinking beer. All the young'uns were in bed, and only the grownups were at the table.

Then Summer came into the bathroom with me and closed the door. Although the cardplayers were making lots of noise when we went in, they got quiet while we were in the bathroom.

"They're listening to us," Summer whispered frantically. "They are trying to hear us go to the bathroom."

"Oh, Summer, that's silly," I said, but I was whispering, too.

About that time the Millers broke into fits of rowdy laughter.

"Three queens!" we heard Mr. Miller holler. "You had three queens all the time!"

"See?" I whispered. "They are payin' us no attention."

Poppy was already in bed, but he came out into the square hallway when he heard us. "I'm glad you're home. I was worried about you."

That was a surprise. He had never said he worried about us before.

"What're you worried for?" Summer said.

"Well," Poppy said, "I was laying there in the bed listening for you, and I got to thinking this is a big city. You don't know what might happen to young girls in big cities."

"Oh."

We had not thought of that. We had never been afraid of the night.

"Promise me you'll try to be home by dark from now on," Poppy said.

We nodded, and Poppy went back to his bed in the kitchen. I went into the bedroom and turned on the light for us. Then Summer came in and we undressed and put on our cotton nightgowns. Summer climbed into bed; then I turned out the light and got in beside her. We didn't speak again. Summer lay on her back by the window, looking at the hazy sky. Hours must have passed when I woke up to find that Summer was moving over the top of me to the other side of the bed.

"Where you goin' to?" I said sleepily.

"Shh . . . shh," she said. "I have to get away from the window."

"What for?"

"It's the searchlights," she whispered as she took my place and pushed me toward the window.

"What about 'em?"

"They're looking for me!"

Looking for her? I was too sleepy to go on with that conversation, so I rolled over and went back to sleep. The next morning when I got up, I found Summer huddled in the corner sleeping underneath the clothes rod, wrapped in a quilt.

five

poppy's check did not come from the mining company back home. The second week of October he got on the telephone down in the Millers' living room and made the first long-distance call of his life.

He hollered into the receiver, "Oliver Altizer!"

Oliver Altizer was a town man.

"This is Claude Compton calling from up here in Flint, Michigan. Did y'all send me my last paycheck?"

"Did you leave your new address with us?" Oliver Altizer said.

" 'Course I did!" Poppy said. "I'm not addled!"

He was upset. He was broke. He had not heard from even one factory.

"I'll have to do some checking," Oliver Altizer told him.

Poppy waited.

"Well, ri'cheer it is, Claude," Oliver Altizer came back. "Did you want me to send it up there to you?"

"What do *you* think?" Poppy snapped.

Oliver Altizer said in a rather cool voice that he would

put the check in the afternoon mail. We would get it in three or four days. Three or four days? There was no money for groceries, nor even for school lunches or Summer's bus fare. We were flat busted.

"We've got flour," Poppy said, and the lines on his forehead were deep. He was worried sick. "And we've got a little milk. You can make biscuits and gravy, can't you, girls?"

I nodded. But Summer wasn't listening. She was sitting at the kitchen table, staring at her hands and laughing softly to herself. Me and Poppy looked at her, then at each other.

Then we shrugged and got back to our money problem. Back home you could just go down to the company store, and they'd give you credit till you were back on your feet.

"What about the rent?" I said. "Will the Millers wait for it?"

"They'll have to," Poppy said as he sat down heavily beside Summer. "Mrs. Miller heard me on the phone. She knows I don't have my check yet. They'll have to wait."

I was thinking about my gym suit, but I didn't mention it. I sat down, too.

"I shoulda been more careful with my spending," Poppy said wearily. "But when we left home I figgered I'd be working for GM by this time."

"How much did that phone call cost?" I said.

"I don't know," Poppy said. "I told Mrs. Miller I'd pay for it when the bill comes."

"What about Henry?" I said. "Would he loan you some money?"

"He's already loaned me money," Poppy said. "Henry's already loaned me money."

He was repeating himself again.

"Don't worry, Poppy," I said. "We'll get by somehow till you get on at a factory."

"I don't know if I'll get on," Poppy said. "That's the problem. I might not get on."

"Why do you say that?" I said. "They need people, don't they?"

"I might be too old," Poppy said. "Henry said I might be too old. They don't hire people over thirty-five 'less they have to."

Poppy was thirty-nine.

"When did he tell you that?" I said.

"The other day. The other day he said I might be too old."

"Well, how come he didn't tell you that sooner?" I hollered. "Now's a fine time to tell you, after we've come all this way. How old is Henry?"

"He's thirty-nine too, but when he came up here they were hiring people over thirty-five. Now they might not be. Henry don't know for sure."

I was mad at Henry. Why hadn't he told us? But if he had, would we have come anyway? It was hard to say.

Summer had her legs crossed, and she was swinging the top one. She was just sitting there, staring at the herbs-and-spices pattern in the oil tablecloth. And her leg kept jerking harder and faster.

"So what are we gonna do?" I said to Poppy.

"I wonder if we've made a mistake," Poppy said. "I wonder if we orta go back home."

"*No!*" Summer wailed suddenly. "We're not going back to that place! I hate that place! If you take me back, I'll kill myself!"

"You hush your mouth!" Poppy said sternly. "I don't wanna hear you sayin' such a thing as that! Besides, I figured you'd be happy to go back home, the way you hate that school."

"I'm not going back!" Summer said again.

"Back where?" I said. "Virginia or school?"

"Neither one! I'm not going back to neither one!"

She put her face in her hands and began to rock back and forth, back and forth, moaning.

"What'chu actin' like this for?" Poppy said to her.

Summer continued to rock and to moan.

The next morning Poppy said we didn't have to go to school until we had the money for lunch and bus fare. Summer lay curled into a ball in the bed, and wouldn't get up.

Me and Poppy took turns washing in the sink. He shaved and dressed in his nice blue slacks and shirt. I put on my best dress. We were going to the grocery store on the corner. It was called Hammady's. We were going to ask for credit. I knew Poppy would rather stick needles in his eyes than do that. But he had to. We had to eat.

Even though it was only October and still warm back

home, it was getting chilly in Michigan, and the radiator had been pumping out heat for more than a week. So we put on our coats, and went to the store.

"I wanna see Mr. Hammady," Poppy said to the clerk. He added "please" as an afterthought.

"Who?" the clerk said. She was just a young girl chewing bubble gum.

"Mr. Hammady, the owner. Ain't this Mr. Hammady's store?"

"Yeah, but he don't stay here. There's a whole bunch of Hammady's stores, Mister. They're all over Flint."

Poppy got red in the face.

"Then who's in charge?" he said. "At this store, I mean? Who's the boss?"

"She is!" the girl said, and pointed to a woman working at a desk in a cubicle beside the front door.

A woman? Well, I'll be dogged.

"Will you tell her I'd like to see her please?" Poppy said.

"What for?" the girl said. She blew a bubble with her gum.

I saw Poppy's face tighten at the girl's rudeness.

"Just tell her, please," he said.

"There's no work here, Mister," the girl said. "So why don'cha move on?"

"I'm not here for work," Poppy said, gritting his teeth. "Please?"

"Mrs. Stiltner!" the girl bellowed.

The woman looked up irritably from her work.

"There's a man here wants to see you!"

Stiltner? That was a back-home name. She motioned us to come over there to the cubicle. We went in. There was one chair, and Mrs. Stiltner motioned Poppy into it. I stood there beside him.

"What can I do for you?" she said wearily, removed her glasses, and rubbed the bridge of her nose.

I looked at Poppy and waited for him to speak. I could see shame casting a shadow on his features.

"My name is Claude Compton," he said. "I just come up here with my two girls from Virginia, and . . ."

"Compton?" Mrs. Stiltner said, and looked at Poppy with more interest. "I used to know some Comptons in Virginia. What part of Virginia?"

"Buchanan County," Poppy said quickly. "I used to know some Stiltners there, too. Are you from there?"

"I shore am," she said with a laugh, and easily slipped back into her mountain accent, which was just like ours.

They were both tickled to death, and started comparing notes about the people they knew. They were people I had heard Poppy talk about from his childhood, but I didn't know them myself. I relaxed. As Poppy and Mrs. Stiltner got more and more friendly and laughed some, I looked at the girl at the cash register. But she wasn't paying us any attention. She was reading a comic book.

"My husband couldn't get on at the factory when we come here," Mrs. Stiltner was saying. " 'Cause of his bad leg. He got a bad leg in the war. I couldn't get him to stay.

He left me last winter. Said he couldn't get used to the cold. So he went back to Virginia."

"You got kids?" Poppy said.

"Two boys, but they're nearabout grown now. One went with his daddy. Paul, the youngest one, he stayed with me. He's seventeen.

"I learned to type in school, so I was able to get a job with Hammady's, and I worked my way up. I like it. It's a good place to work. First I tried to get on at the factory, but they were not hiring women over thirty-five, and I'm thirty-nine."

"What about men?" Poppy said, and it looked like he was holding his breath.

"Oh, they're hiring men of all ages," Mrs. Stiltner said. "You look like a healthy man to me. You'll prob'ly get called soon."

Then they got to the part about us needing credit.

"No problem," Mrs. Stiltner said. "No problem, Mr. Compton. You just pick up what you need. You can charge it."

Then she smiled at me. "And who is this little lady?"

"This is my youngest," Poppy said. "Her name's Lyric. She's in the eighth grade."

"Well, Lyric," Mrs. Stiltner said. "You just pick out anything you want, you heah? I'm always glad to help folks from back home."

We got lots of bananas because Summer liked them, and bacon. She liked bacon, too. Then we got pinto beans and side meat, potatoes, corn meal, canned corn and tomatoes, milk and eggs, and some soap and stuff.

"Git'che some of that candy there, Lyric," Mrs. Stiltner said to me.

She had come over to the cash register when we were checking out.

"I'll take care of it," she went on. "Brenda," she turned to the girl and said, "put Lyric's candy on my account."

"Yes, ma'am," she said.

My eyes met Brenda's as I picked up the candy. She was surprised. Mrs. Stiltner was her boss, and now she was our friend. Bet Brenda wouldn't be so rude to us next time.

Summer was still in bed when we got back. It was after eleven. I went in there and tried to talk to her.

"We got bananas, Summer," I said to her. "And Poppy is going to fix eggs and bacon. I got some candy, too."

She groaned.

"Are you gonna sleep all day?" I said.

She bunched up into a tighter ball and buried her head under the pillow.

"Poppy," I said, when I went back into the kitchen. "What's wrong with her?"

"Who? Summer?" Poppy said, as he laid strips of bacon in the frying pan. "Growin' pains, I reckon."

When the check finally come, Poppy took it down to Hammady's, cashed it, and paid Mrs. Stiltner. Then he paid his other bills, gave me money for my gym suit and lunch money, and Summer lunch money and bus fare.

"I'm not going back to school," Summer said, but she took the money anyway.

" 'Course you are," Poppy said. "You're going back to school tomorrow."

But Poppy was wrong. Summer did not go back to school. Poppy couldn't make her. In fact, he couldn't even make her get out of bed. She slept and slept and slept. She'd get up and eat a little bit. Then go back to bed.

Finally, Poppy said, "All right, Summer, we'll compromise. I'll let you stay home from school this year, if you'll promise to go back next year."

"But then I'll be a year behind," Summer said. "I don't want to be in class with people younger than me."

"Then get up and go to school!" Poppy shouted.

"No, I'm never going back."

Poppy sighed.

"I'm sixteen. You can't make me."

She had a point there.

The next day Summer dressed and went out and found a job washing dishes at a restaurant called Dad's. They were going to pay her fifty cents an hour plus one meal. She came home that day smiling. She was pleased with herself, and we thought now she'll be O.K. Maybe everybody wasn't supposed to go to school. Even if they make straight E's—E stood for Excellent back home—like Summer had always done. Even if they read big fat grownup books and understood every word like Summer did. Maybe she would decide to go back to school later.

The day after that, Poppy was hired at the Chevrolet factory, a part of General Motors, and it was a time of celebration. We could relax. His job was bolting on rearview mirrors. They put him on the second shift, which was two in the afternoon till eleven at night.

"Y'all will have to be here alone in the evenings," he said to me and Summer. "You'll have to fix supper, and look after yourselves. You'll have to call on the Millers if you have any troubles."

"That's fine, Poppy," I said to him. "We can manage."

But Summer was not listening. Once again she was sitting at the kitchen table rocking back and forth, back and forth. She was laughing low to herself, and it looked like she was tickled by the figures in the wallpaper.

six

Me and Summer and Poppy were only three out of thousands of people who came to Flint from the South that year. In their rattletrap cars and trucks they came, packed tight with their two to six young'uns and everything they owned that was any 'count. Or they came like we did on a bus, with everything in a few suitcases. All of us to seek our fortunes.

The Southern people gravitated to the same neighborhoods where you could rent cheap apartments or houses. We huddled together like farm animals in the cold, seeking warmth, comfort, and familiarity with their own kind.

By the time we got there, the stores were already stocked—by popular demand—with dried beans and corn meal, side meat and molasses. They had tons of grits too, but we had never had a bite of grits in our lives, which other Southern folks thought was peculiar. But it was the truth. We had never even seen grits before.

We learned to wear gloves and boots, scarves and earmuffs. We learned to read bus schedules and traffic lights. And we learned to be in the house by five o'clock before the evening fell so dark and cold.

Lives were planned around General Motors. Poppy could count on some days off at Christmas. And two weeks for the changeover at the beginning of July. That's when they'd be setting up the assembly lines for the new models. Maybe we would go back home for a visit with the kinfolks then, Poppy said.

He got double time for working Sundays and holidays. And triple time for working a holiday that fell on a Sunday. He was going to try and work on special days like that. Payday came every other Friday, and that's when you'd see the factory families coming out of their burrows to fight the cold for a while, to buy groceries or shop for bargains.

Where back in the South you might hear, "Are you Republican?" "Are you Baptist?", in Michigan you'd hear, "Are you Union?" And just about everybody was. Poppy became Union, too. The UAW—United Auto Workers— was one of the most powerful unions in the world, he said, and it made a man feel like he had some control over his life to belong. He had to pay dues and go to meetings and fight for more benefits.

In early November two cute young fellers from the Millers' hometown in Louisiana, just discharged from the army, rented the bedroom in the basement. They were trying to get on at a factory, too. Now twelve people lived in the house on Glenwood Avenue.

"We're leaving here soon's I find us another place," Poppy said. "This house is gittin' too crowded."

But there was a housing shortage.

Back home, if you needed a place to live, you just went out and chopped down some trees and built a couple of rooms on the side of the hill that belonged to some of your kinfolks. They might charge you for it and they might not. But if they did, you only had to pay a few dollars for steep land. If it was *real* steep, you could put some stilts under your house. Over the years you'd add a room here, a room there, a bathroom if you were lucky. And eventually you'd have a pretty good place.

But in Flint, Michigan, you couldn't do that. First of all, there was something already built on practically every patch of land in sight. Second, you couldn't chop down a tree. They were all in somebody's yard. And third, you had to have a thing called a building permit even to tack a porch on to your place.

There was an article in the *Flint Journal* about people taking advantage of the poor moving up from the South, charging them high rent for practically nothing, and putting too many people in a house. They didn't say anything about people from the South, like the Millers, taking advantage of their own kind. Until then I had not realized we were poor. We had never seemed poor before, but now I could see where it might look that way to Yankees.

Summer was happy with her job, and with the money she was making. She took a fancy to one of the ex-soldiers in the basement. His name was Bill. When she got off work, she hung around outside in the cold, just to see him come and go. When she saw him, she flirted with him, and he talked to her, but he didn't ask her for a date. I heard him tell his buddy he knew better than to date young girls.

"Yeah, 'cause her daddy would prob'ly kill you!" the other feller said with a chuckle.

I told Summer what I heard, but she didn't give up. She started spending all her money from Dad's on lipstick and makeup and new dresses.

Then her face broke out. Summer had always been fair-complected, but now the pinkness turned to red and was covered with pimples. She was frantic.

"Oh, no," she wailed in front of the mirror over the sink. "Just look at me. I'm ugly! I'm so ugly!"

"Will you quit pickin' at it!" Poppy hollered at her. "Just leave it alone, and stop that moanin' and groanin'. Dab some Noxzema on your face every night, and quit pickin' at it, and it'll be all right. Your mama used Noxzema from the time she was sixteen till the day she died and she never had a pimple—not the first one."

So Summer used Noxzema every night, but she couldn't stop picking at her face. She'd pick a place till it bled, and natur'ly you're gonna keep sores on your face if you can't leave them alone.

"I can't help it!" she told Poppy. "I forget. I start thinking about something, and I forget what I'm doing. It's just a habit."

She was right about that. I watched her. At night she sat

by the window not doing anything, just sitting there, sometimes with a secret smile on her face, and swinging her leg, faster and harder, and picking at her face. It got worse and worse. It got so bad she stopped going out a'tall. She was afraid Bill might see her. She went back to bed and stayed there. After a few days of this, the restaurant called Mrs. Miller's house, and somebody hollered up the stairs.

"Summer Compton! You up there?"

But Summer didn't answer. She hid her head down under the covers and wouldn't even peep out.

"Summer Compton! Dad's called and wanted to know if you are coming back to work."

"Tell them no," I answered for Summer. "She's sick."

Somebody downstairs snorted. "Sick, my hind end!"

Dad's didn't call again, and Summer's last paycheck was mailed to her. She didn't work anywhere after that.

I got the bright idea of putting thin cotton gloves on Summer's hands so she wouldn't forget and pick at her face. And she said it was O.K. She wore the gloves all the time, and her face began slowly to heal, but she had scars. Her days of pretty complexion were over.

seven

At school we had debates in Social Studies class about integration. I didn't know what that word meant till I listened to the debates for a while. Then I figured it out.

What surprised me was that my classmates were all saying they did not want to go to school with colored children. No matter where they were raised, they said that. Some had lived in Michigan all their lives.

They said, "I'm not prejudiced, *but* I think we should be separate but equal." Or, "I'm not prejudiced, *but* I think they should have their own neighborhoods and their own schools."

And I had always figured up-North folks were so open-minded. In fact, before I came here, I had thought all the schools and neighborhoods would be mixed. But I was wrong. There were no colored children in Zimmerman Junior High, nor even in our neighborhood.

I didn't join the debates, because I was too bashful. I just listened. But I did have some opinions of my own, and I debated in my head.

Everybody talked about the South like it was brimming over with colored folk, and you couldn't go anywhere without running into one. Actually, in my whole life I had not seen a colored person in the flesh until I was on my way to Flint. Still, I knew in my heart of hearts that colored folks were just like me, no better and no worse. I don't know how I knew. I just did. They were people like me.

And I figured when people say, "I'm not prejudiced, *but* . . . ," that means they really *are* prejudiced, and they are just trying to find a way to make it O.K. So I would say to myself I am *not* prejudiced, and there's no *but*s about it.

I decided I would tell the class all of that one of these days. But when the teacher, Mr. Pinkney, finally did call on me for my opinion, I couldn't speak. I just turned red, and looked at my hands and felt their eyes on me for what seemed like a long, long time, until finally he moved on to somebody else.

Then Mr. Pinkney talked to us about how important it is to think for yourself and not be influenced by the attitudes of other people, no matter who they are. He said you shouldn't never accept what somebody says just 'cause they said it. You should question things.

"Other people's attitudes sometimes seep into our thoughts by osmosis," he went on, and we all knew what that meant, 'cause we'd been reading about osmosis in Science. "We absorb them, and we start to think these are our own thoughts. That's how, if we're not alert, we let other people do our thinking for us. And unscrupulous people can get control of our minds in that way."

After class that day a girl named Yolanda came up to me at my locker, where I was whirling the dial on my combination lock like I'd been doing it all my life. She was a dark-haired beauty. She had what they call "snapping black eyes" in *True Story Magazine*, perfect straight teeth, and rosy cheeks. In fact, I had eyed her lots of times when she didn't know it, and I had thought that's what I would pick to look like if I had a choice in the matter.

"You don't feel that way about colored people, do you?" she asked.

I shook my head.

"Me neither," she said.

It was the beginning of our friendship, and I was thrilled that a girl like Yolanda would be friendly with me. Our walk home took us in the same direction.

"My mama is dead, too," she told me. "My daddy and me, we came up here from Texas last year."

I reckoned her Southern drawl was worse than mine.

"Do you remember your mama?" I asked.

"Oh, yeah, she only died two years ago."

"I don't remember my mama, but I wisht I did," I said.

"I'll tell you a secret," Yolanda said and put her lips near my ear. "Promise you won't tell?"

"Sure," I agreed.

You'd think we'd been buddies for years.

"My mama was a colored woman," she whispered.

"Then how come you ain't colored?" I said.

"She was *half* colored. Her daddy was white, and her

mama was colored. And my own daddy is full-blooded Mexican. I take after him. I don't tell everybody 'bout Mama 'cause they start treatin' me different soon's they find out. And you know something, Lyric? They peck you to death when you're different."

I just looked at her.

"Back in Texas, I usta have chickens. They were just your ordinary run o' the mill, cluckin', squawkin', egg-layin' chickens, you know? But I liked 'em.

"And then this solid white one come along. I called her Opal. She was so pretty. But the other chickens ganged up on Opal and pecked, pecked, pecked at 'er. They woulda killed her too, if I hadn't took up for her."

What she was saying that day, I didn't get right then, and I didn't know what to say. So I didn't say anything, 'cause I had learned from reading Mark Twain that it's better to keep your mouth shut and appear stupid, than to open it and remove all doubt. I had been reminded of that lesson quite often since coming to Michigan.

"I can go down Glenwood Avenue with you," she offered when we were nearing our parting of the ways. "Then I can cut over to West Court. That's where I live."

But I didn't want her to see our house. I was afraid she might drop in sometime, and I was ashamed of the apartment. I would ask her over when Poppy found us a better place to live.

"Oh, I have to stop at the drugstore today," I lied, "and pick up some things for Poppy."

And I thought I was saved.

But she said, "I'll go to the drugstore with you."

"O.K.," I said lamely. "Don't your daddy expect you home?"

"He's on the second shift. Nobody's home."

"Same here," I said.

Somewhere in the back of my head I wondered why I had said that. Summer was home. She was somebody. Was I ashamed of her, too?

We went into the drugstore at the corner where West Court and Glenwood came together, and I moved around amongst the shelves, thinking I would buy some lil' ole something we needed, but it would have to be *real* little, 'cause I didn't have much money with me.

"Wanna get a soda?" Yolanda said.

"Sure," I agreed, and we went to the counter, perched upon the stools, and told the soda jerk to give us fountain cherry Cokes.

He was a young feller. And he was plainly smitten with Yolanda. He couldn't keep his eyes off of her.

"Wanna play the jukebox?" Yolanda said to me, not paying him a bit of attention.

"Sure," I agreed again, and we went over to the jukebox to see what they had.

"I just love this one," Yolanda said, and she punched "Moments to Remember" by the Four Lads.

We sat back down and listened. It had the sweetest harmony, which Yolanda appreciated as much as I did. It also had pretty words, which I memorized.

Though summer turns to winter
And the present disappears
The laughter we were glad to share
Will echo through the years.

Then we played another song and sipped on our drinks, and talked some more. The soda jerk got to talking to us, nobody else came into the store, and I was happy. It smelled like vanilla extract in there, and it was so cozy and cheerful I lost track of the time.

When I looked out and saw how dark it was, I like to died. Summer was alone with nobody to turn on a light for her!

"Oh, Yolanda!" I said. "I gotta go! It's dark out there!"

"Yeah, it gets dark so early nowadays," she said. "But what about your daddy's stuff you were supposed to get?"

"It can wait," I mumbled. "I gotta go."

And I rushed out and down the street.

As I got up close to the house I could see a flickering glow in the kitchen. What could that be? I hurried up the stairs calling Summer's name. I was breathing so fast.

"I'm here, Summer! I'm home!"

"In the kitchen, Lyric!" she called out excitedly. "Come see!"

The flickering I had seen from the street was coming from a candle. Summer had perched it and lit it in the middle of the table, and she was standing there over it.

"What'chu doin'?" I said.

"Oh, look, Lyric! See how big I am!"

She was bending her body up and down, up and down over the candle, and the light threw a creepy black shadow of her all over the room. The shadow was normal-sized when she moved away from the candle, but when she got closer to the light, it loomed up bigger and bigger until it covered the whole ceiling and the walls.

"I am a giant!" she squealed. "Lookit! Lookit! I am big! The candle makes me so big!"

I was relieved she wasn't upset. I tossed my books on Poppy's cot and watched her move back and forth, back and forth again and again, giggling and clapping her hands like a little girl.

"I am big, Lyric! I am big!"

And I had a sudden memory of me and Summer at the county fair two or three years ago, and we were riding on the Ferris wheel. We were both so happy that day.

Eating cotton candy high over a crowd of mountain people, Summer had looked down at them and squealed, "See how little they are, Lyric! They look like ants, and we are big! We are *so* big!"

eight

A few days later, when I got home, Summer was not laughing. She was pacing, pacing, pacing in the kitchen.

"It's about time you got here," she said to me real hateful. "I been all by myself again. It's Poppy's day off and he went someplace with that Stiltner woman from the store!"

"Mrs. Stiltner?" I said. I was tickled. "Well, ain't that something? Did you see her?"

"No, he was meeting her at the store."

Summer went on pacing. Back and forth. Back and forth. From the window to the door and back again. It was about eight steps.

"He shouldn't be courtin'!" she said hotly, and folded her arms across her chest.

"Why not?" I said. "I think it's nice."

"No!" Summer said and stomped her foot hard on the kitchen floor. "No, it's *not* nice!"

"What's wrong with it?" I said. "Mrs. Stiltner's man left

her. They been separated a year now. She's thirty-nine years old, and so's Poppy. He ain't had a girlfriend since Mama died, and . . ."

"Mama is *not* dead!" Summer screamed.

The most peculiar thing was not what she said but how she said it. She made the words come out shrill and loud, but the expression on her face didn't change, and she didn't fling her arms around or anything. It seemed like the sound came from somebody else, maybe a monster, way down deep inside her, and she had nothing to do with it.

The scream echoed in the room as I took some cold biscuits, parked at the table, and started nibblin'. I didn't have much of an appetite. I was thinking of all the idiotic things Summer had done since we got to Michigan. Yeah, I thought, *idiotic* was the word, but it was that bloodcurdling scream of hers that gave me goose bumps.

Mama is not dead? I faced it right then. Something was bad wrong with Summer. She stood there for a moment perfectly still. Then she went back to pacing, and babbling.

"I told him. I told him not to go. I told him you'd be mad. I told him. I did my part. Jibble, jibble."

Jibble, jibble?

I watched her. Her face was better, but not normal yet. Her hands were bare, but during the time she had been wearing the gloves, she'd let her fingernails grow out. Now they were awful long and dirty. She had on a ratty old housecoat, and her hair was hanging in her face in dirty strands. She hadn't washed it or even combed it for some time.

Seeing her every day I had not noticed what a great big change this was from her old self. But if somebody from back home saw Summer right then, I'll declare they wouldn't have even recognized her as that same bright-eyed little gal she usta be. They might have even thought she was some crazy woman.

"He won't listen to me. You'll have to tell him. When he comes home, jibble, you tell him," she went on.

I spoke up then. "You talking to me, Summer?"

"No!" she screamed. "You stay out of this. It's none of your business."

"Then who're you talking to?"

"Mama!" she screamed again. "I was telling Mama what Poppy's done! Don't you know that? Oh, he thought he could get away with this! But he can't. I told!"

"Summer," I said. "Where is Mama?"

"She's ri'cheer, Lyric!" Summer said and pointed to the air in front of her. She said it like I was slow in the head, and she had lost patience with me. "Right beside Grandpa!"

I would have laughed then if she hadn't been so pathetic.

"Grandpa?" I said. "He's not dead either?"

"Yeah," Summer said more calmly as she sat down beside me. "Yeah, Grandpa's dead, jibble, jibble."

"Summer, what do you mean by that . . . that jibble?"

"Jibble, jibble," she said.

"Jibble is not a word, Summer."

"It is my word, Lyric—*my* word," she went on. "It is not yours! And you know what else? It was that foreman's fault, jibble. Grandpa told me if that foreman hadn't a'said what he did, well, you know, Grandpa might've lived."

It was funny she should say that. I had often thought of it myself, but never would I mention such a thing out loud. I hadn't heard anybody else say it either. That foreman could very well have made a mistake in his calculations. And if he hadn't told those miners they had only one hour to live, then our grandpa might've been rescued right along with the others.

"I think that's the truth," I said seriously to Summer. "That foreman was just an educated idiot who orta kept his mouth shut. Then everybody—including Grandpa—could've gone on hoping."

Summer seemed satisfied with that. She sat at the table with me while I ate, and she didn't talk to Mama anymore. But she didn't talk to me either. I tried to say things about school, but her mind was somewheres else again, and after a while she got up and left the room right in the middle of my talking. Then I could hear her in the bedroom whispering, whispering . . . jibble, jibble . . .

I decided it was time for me and Poppy to have a serious talk about this stuff Summer was doing. He came home about nine, smelling of cooked onions and tobacco. Summer was in bed. I was sitting at the kitchen table studying. He kissed me on top of my head.

"What'chu learnin'?" he said.

"The minor keys," I said.

"The whichum?" he said and looked at my music book, which was open in front of me.

"The Michigan kids have been studying music theory all the years they've been in school," I said. "And I was way behind, but I'm almost up with them now."

"I never learned any of that stuff," Poppy said as he picked up his guitar. "But it never stopped me from playing any song I heard."

"Yeah, but most folks can't do that, Poppy."

Softly he began to pluck out the notes to "Wildwood Flower."

"Have fun tonight?" I said.

"It was all right. I met Gayle's boy, Paul. He's a right nice young feller."

Poppy began to sing.

I'll twine 'mid the ringlets of my raven black hair
With the roses so red and the lilies so fair
The myrtle so green of an emerald hue
The pale morning glory with eyes of bright blue.

That song always brought dreamy images to my mind. I could see that sad-eyed little thing way back there in the hills a long time ago. Maybe she was one of the first settlers in the Appalachians, except for the Indians. Or maybe *she* was Indian, 'cause she talks about her raven-black hair. Anyhow, she's sitting there alone in a deep holler, plaiting wildflowers into her long hair, and this song comes to her mind, born from her grief and longing. She never imagined it would echo its way down through the generations.

I added my alto to Poppy's baritone melody.

He taught me to love him, and promised to love
Through ill and misfortune, all others above
But I woke from my dreaming, my idol was clay
My visions of love have all faded away.

I'll think of him never, I'll be wildly gay
I'll charm every heart, and drive troubles away
I'll live yet to see him regret this dark hour
When he won and neglected his frail wildwood flower.

Our pleasant song suddenly ended in discord and racket as Poppy let out a cry and tossed his treasured guitar onto the floor with a loud ker-boom and an echo of vibrating strings.

My eyes went to the doorway where Poppy was looking. Summer was standing there in her nightgown with bloody scratches on her face. We both rushed to her side.

"Oh, my darlin' girl!" Poppy said. "What's happened to you?"

"See what they did to me," she said softly.

"Summer, what happened?" I cried out.

"They scratched me. They wanted to taste my blood," she said, still calm and controlled.

"Who? What on earth do you mean?" Poppy said.

"The wolves were here," Summer said. "They did this to me."

Me and Poppy were stunned. We couldn't even move for a few seconds, then we sprung into action at the same time.

"Come sit at the table," Poppy said, as he led her there.

I got a clean cloth and dabbed at her wounds. I could see that the scratches were not very deep, but one had grazed the corner of her right eye.

Summer just sat there, serene and still at last, with the palms of her hands turned upward on her knees. You could see the blood layered above the dirt underneath her long fingernails.

"Go down and ask the Millers to fetch a doctor for us," Poppy said quietly to me.

And I scurried down the stairs.

But in Michigan you couldn't fetch a doctor to save your life. You had to go to him. The Millers told me that and followed me back up the stairs.

"Did you call the doctor?" Poppy said, when we entered the kitchen. He was sitting by Summer with one arm around her.

"What happened?" Mr. Miller said.

"She hurt her eye," Poppy said. "Is the doctor coming or not?"

"Doctors don't come to you here, but we'll take her to the emergency room for you," Mrs. Miller said.

"Oh," Poppy said. "All right." Then he turned to me. "Get her coat, will you, Lyric? And her shoes."

57

I rushed into our room, found Summer's coat, shoes, and socks and returned to the kitchen. Then me and Poppy put on Summer's things for her, while she just sat there, limp and dazed, still in her nightgown under the coat. When I looked at the Millers again, I found them in the same position, staring at Summer. They didn't know what to say.

Poppy put his own coat back on, and we led Summer down the stairs. The Millers got together their coats and car keys while me and Poppy huddled with Summer at the front door. Then the grownups led her out to the car.

Nobody said it, but I knew it was my place to stay with the Miller children, who were sleeping. I stood at the front window, clutching the ledge and looking after the car long after it was out of sight.

They treated Summer's wounds, then put her in the psychiatric ward at Hurley Hospital and kept her there for three days before they let anybody see her. Poppy paced the floor and acted about as crazy as Summer. He blamed his own self for what happened, saying if he'd stayed home with her she'd be all right.

"I won't leave her alone no more," he said.

But in all our years together I couldn't remember Poppy ever neglecting us in any way. This was not his fault. So I tried to tell him that. Still he beat up on himself.

"I knew she wadn't acting right, and I had no business traipsing off to have a good time," he said.

When Poppy was allowed to see her, I couldn't go with

him. It was no place to take a thirteen-year-old girl, they said.

Poppy was even more shook up after he saw Summer. He said it really was the awfullest place, and he couldn't hardly stand to see his sweet girl left there. He said people were screamin' and cussin', and some of them were in straitjackets 'cause you couldn't turn 'em loose. But Summer just lay there, very still, and she didn't seem to care about anything.

They had forced her into a hot bath, Poppy told me, where they had cut her fingernails, and also cut her hair real short and washed it. Then they had put her in a white hospital gown, treated the eye, and dabbed some purple medicine on her face, but didn't bandage it. They had to tie her hands to the bed to keep her from picking at the scratches.

"I never seed anything so pitiful in my life," Poppy said with a quiver in his voice. "It didn't look like our Summer a'tall. And if her name hadn't been on the bed chart, I wouldn't a'known who it was."

He was so hurt and sad, I'll declare I don't know how Poppy went on working, but he felt like he had to. He said his girls needed him to keep on working now more than ever.

"They're saying Summer thinks things are after her. And she's got delusions and hallucinations," Poppy told me. "She thinks she sees the dead. She's gone mental, and that's all there is to it."

"Couldn't they tell you something we didn't already know?" I said, not meaning to be sarcastic. But it was the truth.

"The mind is a complicated and mysterious thing, Lyric, my girl. And I'll declare, as good as the doctors are, I don't think they know a lot about it."

Then he put his head in his hands and said a prayer of thanks to Jesus for General Motors and that good hospitalization policy they gave him. Because, otherwise, what on earth would become of his Summer?

"They've put her on some real powerful medicine," he went on, "and she's calmed down for now."

nine

On December 23, Poppy brought Summer home—a zombie. She gave me a shadow of a smile when she first came in, but she didn't smile again for a spell. You could see the red streaks all down her face where she had scratched herself. Her right eye had a big blood spot in the white part. Her fingernails were short, but I put the white gloves back on her anyway, and she didn't object.

She took her pills like she was supposed to, then she sat there in the kitchen and looked out the window. The medicine made her sluggish, and she moved in slow motion.

I fixed meals, and she ate when I called her to the table. She spoke hardly at all, and when she did, her speech was slow. Her words came out slurred like she couldn't get her mouth open wide enough to make the right sounds. She told me when she needed to go to the bathroom, and most times I went with her, not just to turn on the light, but because she seemed so helpless.

———

On Christmas Eve, heavy gray snow clouds gathered all day and dumped their load by nightfall. And such a snow! A stark white beauty transformed Glenwood Avenue, covering the shabbiness. It was a miracle out there under the streetlamps.

Summer sat by the window and watched. I kept thinking, *Silent night, holy night . . .*

I carried a cup of cocoa to her on a saucer. "Want a marshmallow?" I asked softly, placing the saucer into her hands.

"No."

I sat down with her. With our heads together we sipped and looked out at the cold night, wordless.

Indoors, it was not a Christmas you would dream about. No stockings hung over the fireplace. We didn't have a fireplace. Not even a chimney. No excited previous days full of shopping and planning. No breathless whispered secrets and giggles. No decorations on the front porch, which wasn't even ours to decorate. No reindeer. I remembered Christmases back home when we had all of those things, and I felt an ache around my heart.

Poppy had given me a few dollars, which I had spent hurriedly at the drugstore one evening before darkness fell. There were a few presents under a pitiful tree in the corner. A few goodies in the ancient refrigerator, and on the table. Only a hope and a promise that this was temporary. Next year would be better. That was the gift we gave to each other.

Next year we'll live in a house, I thought.

Next year we'll have a big tree with lights.

And presents and a ham.

Next year she'll be well again.

Poppy was out doing some last-minute shopping with Henry. He had promised to be home by eight. Earlier in the evening we'd eaten a small supper I had fixed. In Michigan you didn't have to buy a whole turkey. You could buy only a part. So that's what we did. We had bought a small breast of turkey, and cranberry sauce in a jar. I had made gravy, biscuits, and mashed potatoes, and heated up canned green beans. We had store-bought pumpkin pie, and it was good. We had all eaten until we were stuffed, even Summer.

"When is Poppy coming home?" she asked now.

Again she sounded like a child.

"Soon."

Some people were strolling down the sidewalk in the snow, singing carols.

"That's a tradition here," I said to Summer. "People go up and down the street singing carols on Christmas Eve."

You couldn't do that back home, I was thinking. In the hollers there was no good place to walk. And you didn't have any lights. You were liable to fall down the creek bank in the dark. And the houses were too far apart. You might have to walk for miles. Yeah, caroling was definitely a city tradition.

"Maybe we could do it next year," Summer said.

"Yeah, we can," I said brightly. "We'll plan on it."

We watched the snow some more.

"Remember that movie we saw last year?" I said. "The one with Bing Crosby? *White Christmas*?"

She turned to me then with that ghost of a smile. "Yeah, I remember."

"Remember the song we learned—'Sisters'?"

"Yeah, I do."

"Let's sing it now."

"O.K."

We played around with the notes for a minute, trying to find the right key. Then it came.

> *Those who've seen us*
> *Know there's not a thing*
> *Can come between us!*

It felt so right to sing in harmony with her again. Her words came out more distinct when she sang, and her voice was as good as ever, which was far better than most folks'.

> *Lord, help the mister*
> *Who comes between me and my sister!*
> *And Lord help the sister*
> *Who comes between me and my man!*

"Let's do a Christmas carol now," she said then.

"O.K., which one?"

"When flowers blossomed mid the snow . . ." she sang in her clear high voice, so like a bell, and I joined in with my alto.

> *. . . Upon a winter's night,*
> *Was born a child, the Christmas rose,*
> *The king of love and light!*

After that, we sang some more songs before Poppy came home. We could hear his footsteps on the stairs, and we began to sing "Lo, How a Rose E'er Blooming." It was his favorite. He took off his coat and boots. He had an air of cold about him. His cheeks were red and his hands were chapped, and he rubbed them together.

He placed two beautifully wrapped presents under the tree real careful, then stood there smiling at us as we sang in that dingy little kitchen. I knew his heart was full at seeing Summer singing again, and I knew he was thinking about us—his girls. His songbirds, as he usta call us. His life. We always knew we were loved. Always.

Just stood there, he did, and listened to us sing on Christmas Eve, as the snow threw a merciful blanket over us, and gave us this bittersweet Christmas together.

ten

beginning the first of January, Summer went to see a psychiatrist every Tuesday and Friday morning at eleven o'clock. That was right when I went to Mr. Buell's English class, and I would look at the clock on the wall and think of her, and wonder what she was saying to the doctor.

Was she talking about our life together way back there in the bottom between the hills? Was the doctor seeing into that head of hers and figuring out what made her go mental? We had the same childhood. Did they know how come she had so much fear in her that I didn't have? What was it that haunted her so?

There was such a big sadness in our Summer that you couldn't even comprehend the depth of it. I would ask her about her visits to the doctor, but she didn't want to talk about it. I kept thinking of the Bible verse, *"Yea, though I walk through the valley of the shadow of death . . ."* It seemed like that was where my sister was at—in the valley of the shadow of death. And when I remembered the happy-birthday face from last August—only five months ago—I wondered if I would ever see it again.

One night I had a strange dream.

Me and Summer are walking up Glory Bottom. We are barefooted. It is dark and we are afraid, so we hurry, holding on to each other. The holler is deeper, colder, more isolated than I remember it ever being. The hills are taller, the woods thicker. Rolling purplish black clouds are moving in the sky over us. Moving, moving, rumbling . . . rumbling . . .

"We'll be home soon, Summer," I whisper. "Hold on to me."

And then there are green eyes in the dark behind us. And there are huge paws hitting heavy on the packed-down dirt, and there are panting sounds. It's wolves after us, big black wolves with long sharp teeth, nipping at our heels.

"Run, Summer! Run!"

And we run together, unable to see the road, not knowing how close we are to the creek bank. And suddenly I sprout wings, and I lift myself up a few feet off the road. Still I hold on to Summer.

"Come on, Summer, fly!"

"I can't. I can't fly! I can't get my feet off the ground!"

"Sure you can. It's easy. Just jump up into the air like this."

And I am flying, flying, but I am still holding on to Summer, trying to help her lift off. The wolves are closing in. We can hear them growling and feel their hot breath.

"Don't leave me, Lyric! Please don't leave me behind!"

But I am terrified. I let go of Summer. I let go and I fly away.

I woke up with a cry.

Oh, Summer, Summer, I had to let go . . .

Our bedroom was very dark. I looked out at the night sky and tried to calm my racing heart. I could hear Summer's deep breathing beside me.

"Thank you, God, it's not real. Thank you, God, it was only a dream."

It was that kind of dream. That kind of feeling. Just too awful to dwell on, so you try to forget it.

At breakfast Poppy asked Summer in his quiet way how she had slept, and she said, "I had a bad dream."

"A nightmare?" Poppy said gently.

"Yeah, a nightmare. The wolves again," she said, and her voice was tiny and weak like a child's. "In Glory Bottom, they were after me."

"And what happened?" I said, holding my breath.

"I don't remember," she said. "I just don't remember. But I don't want to talk about it no more."

I did a lot of thinking about that, and I couldn't explain it, but I felt that maybe me and Summer had dreamed the same dream again. Only I remembered how it ended. And I figured God had given me this little bitty taste of Summer's terror so I'd understand. And I did understand. I understood that she was in a nightmare she couldn't wake up from.

eleven

At school I learned to say "ree-al-lee," and "yous guys" instead of "y'all." Don't ask me why yous guys is more proper than y'all. I don't know.

I learned not to jump out of my desk and run to the window when an airplane flew over so low you could read the numbers on the wings. I had done that once, saying, "Looky yonder, would'ja?" And for some reason I thought everybody else would jump up too, but I was wrong.

Dewey the heckler had said, "Hillbilly, hillbilly," low under his breath as I went back to my seat with a red face. So I learned to ignore planes that acted like they wanted to land on the roof, even if I was itching to go see.

I had learned not to say, "I'm give out," after running laps around the gym. And I had also learned not to say "Tarnation!" when somebody told what the temperature was, even though I had never before seen the mercury in a thermometer drop so low.

The cold was bitter and brutal. It got way down in your bones, and you couldn't get away from it.

By the time I walked to Zimmerman from home, that bare place on my legs between the top of my boots and the hem of my dress was numb. Girls were not allowed to wear slacks to school. It made me mad to be so cold when I could look around me and see the boys had their legs all covered up in corduroy or wool, warm as toast.

"What's the problem with slacks?" I said angrily to Yolanda, Gladys, and Nadine as we were going into Mrs. Gaspar's first-period music class one morning. We four had become pretty good friends by then. "I can't feel my legs!"

"It's not ladylike," Gladys said sarcastically.

"Well, it's not ladylike to freeze your legs off either!" I said.

"No, 'cause then you have to walk around on your butt!" Yolanda said.

My mad spell evaporated as we all busted out laughing. Mrs. Gaspar tried to call the class to order, but we were hysterical.

"What's so funny?" she said, but we couldn't even speak. "Lyric, see me after class. Maybe you can find your voice by then."

Just Lyric? What was fair about that? Now I was mad again. Seeing Mrs. Gaspar after class probably meant detention. I had it all planned how I would tell her she was unfair. How come she picked me out of that group of four?

But when I went up to her desk after class with all that rebellion puffing me up, she knocked the wind out of my sails.

"You know I don't want you to make a habit of this, Lyric, but it's good to see you laughing. You usually seem sad."

Nobody had ever told me that before. Back home, folks said I could light up a room. But maybe it was not so anymore. I didn't know what to say.

"Are you homesick?" she went on.

I thought about it.

"Once in a while," I replied.

"What do you miss most?" Mrs. Gaspar said, giving me her complete and undivided attention. She was a pretty lady, with nice blond hair and blue eyes. She played the piano, and she knew everything there was to know about music.

"I guess I miss Summer the most," I said wistfully.

And that was double-talk. Only Mrs. Gaspar didn't know it.

"Oh, the cold weather makes you feel sad?" she said kindly.

I shrugged and said, "Not sad exactly. But I can't help remembering how things usta be."

I thought the world and all of Mrs. Gaspar, and she wasn't just nodding her head and thinking of other things like some teachers do. She was really listening to me; but somehow I just couldn't tell her about Summer.

After a little while she gave me a pass for my next class so I wouldn't get a tardy mark, and I went on.

I realized that somewheres back in those hills I had absorbed this attitude—like Mr. Pinkney's osmosis—that insanity was one of those skeletons you wanted to keep in the closet.

I remembered the Moore family who lived way high on a mountaintop. They had a crazy aunt who sat in a rocking chair on the porch all the time and hollered out nasty things. They called her Sadie. If somebody chanced to go by the house, which was not too often, they jerked Sadie inside and closed the door. When you did something dumb, folks were apt to call you Sadie.

Then there was Billie Shell. He was really nutty. They kept him hid as long as they could, but they finally had to send him off to the lunatic asylum.

And I thought of all the sayings people have for the mentally ill. Words I had picked up myself. Crazy. Nuts. She's got a screw loose. He lost his marbles. Batty. Lunatic. Looney.

That day after school I went to the grocery store because there were things we needed and couldn't do without another day. Like soap and potatoes. Sure, I got some pop too, but I was there anyways, and I wouldn't have gone just for pop. I wouldn't have gone just for the Cracker Jacks either. And I did get Summer some bananas. So I really was thinking of her.

I hurried as fast as I could, but it got dark on me before I could get home. I rushed up the steps, hauling groceries and calling for Summer. I lost my breath doing it, but she was not in the apartment!

I dumped my pokes on the table. I was scared to death. Where was she? I had heard Poppy make her promise she wouldn't go anywhere from the time he went to work till I got home. When I came straight from school, it was not a long time for her to sit beside the window and wait, like she promised she would.

With my heart flying, I went running down the stairs again. The Millers were out, and the house seemed empty and spooky. It echoed. I found her standing right outside the bathroom in the dark in a puddle. She had wet herself.

"I wanted to go in and turn on the light all by myself," she said in her tiny voice. She sounded like a mouse squeaking. "I was determined. It wasn't all the way dark then, but . . . but I couldn't, Lyric. I was too skeerd to go in and flip on the switch. I froze up."

So she had stood outside the door, and couldn't move. But she couldn't hold it in either.

I thought about her wanting to go in the bathroom and turn on the light by herself. She had never done that before, and it was like something inside her was telling her it was a matter of life and death, but still she couldn't do it.

My mind went to those happy Saturdays back home, sitting in a dark movie theater with Summer. There was a particular scene we had seen maybe fifty times in different movies. You know the one where somebody is hanging off a cliff or a window ledge. Just hanging there, screaming and yelling for help. Then along comes another person. Maybe it's a cowboy on a horse, or some other hero, and he hollers, "Hold on!"

Me and Summer made fun every single time we heard that. And we'd talked about it more than once, wondering if a person couldn't think of something more useful to say under those circumstances. Like, "I'm gittin' you a rope," or "I'm puttin' a horse under you." Or a mattress, or a haystack. Whatever.

But, hold on?

But now that's what I wanted to say to Summer—"Hold on!" And I knew it was useless, because just like the figure on the cliff, she already *was* holding on for dear life.

Without a word I cleaned up the floor and helped her clean herself, and then I led her back to the apartment. She stopped on the stairs, did a slow turn, and looked at me. Her face was miserable.

"What's wrong with me, Lyric?" she whispered.

"I don't know, Summer."

"Will I get better?"

"Sure you will. You're gonna get all better real soon."

"I hope so." She said it tired and slow. "It'll have to be soon, or it'll be too late."

"Too late?"

"Yeah, 'cause I think I'm disappearing, Lyric. I'm just . . . disappearing."

We went on up the stairs, and I tried not to stare at her. But I couldn't help it. Her eyes darted around constantly. They didn't usta do that. Her fingers fluttered like crippled birds. She moved slow. She was bent over. She was troubled. *She looked old.*

———

I waited up for Poppy to get home from work. I told him what had happened, and that strange thing Summer had said. He was buttering a piece of corn bread, and his knife stopped in mid-air like it forgot what to do next.

"Disappearing?" he whispered. Then he laid the knife down on the plate real gentle and his bread beside it. "Yeah, Lyric, I know that's how she feels. She told me her shadow had left her."

"She thinks she has no shadow?"

"That's what she thinks," Poppy said sadly.

I recalled it was her shadow that made her so big on the walls and ceiling that night. Now she thought it was gone.

Poppy just sat there with his hands folded up under his chin and his elbows propped on the table, staring at his plate. Seemed like his appetite had left him.

I went to bed then, and a couple of hours passed, I reckon, when I woke up to the sound of the hall window going up. I turned my head toward Summer and saw that she was sleeping soundly. The medicine did that for her.

I listened to her deep breathing for a moment. I remembered how she had once said to me, "Did you ever think what a mysterious thing sleep is? You go down deep inside yourself, you know. You go in there and you talk to another you. And together y'all figure out how you're gonna do things the next day. That's what sleeping's all about. It's time out to plan your strategy."

Well, it was for sure she needed all the strategy she could get right now, so I was careful not to disturb her as I slipped out of bed, wrapped myself up in a blanket, put on my shoes, and went into the hallway. A blast of cold air hit me in the face. The window was open, and I could see Poppy standing on the roof in his overcoat. He was taking in the peace of the night. I closed the bedroom door behind me real quiet, climbed out there, and stood beside him. He put an arm across my shoulder and smiled down at me.

The cold weather seemed to have cleared up the haze that usually lay over the city, and we just stood there together looking at the royal-blue sky with a bright bold moon shining on the snow and ice. There were a trillion stars.

"Can't sleep?" I whispered to Poppy.

"No, too much on my mind," he said.

There was ice on the roof, and if you didn't watch out, you could go sliding down over the side. So we stood in the same spot, without moving.

"Poppy, you worried 'bout Summer?"

He gave a long heavy sigh. "Yeah, a wise man once said, 'Why worry when you can pray?', but somehow I can't help it. I keep wishing your mama was here to tell me what to do."

"I don't reckon there's much you *can* do," I whispered. "Can you?"

He was silent.

"Poppy, do you think she woulda been all right if we'd stayed put back home?"

"You mean if she'd married Anderson Biddle and got

half of the A&P?" Poppy said, and looked down at me. I could tell his eyes were twinkling.

We laughed softly together.

"No, that would drive anybody crazy," I said. "But do you think moving up here made her sick?"

Poppy sighed again. "No, Lyric. I asked the doctor that same thing. And I asked him if I took her home would she be all right again, and he said no. He said there's always been this dormant seed in Summer's mind. And he said the move to Michigan might've triggered it to come alive, but if we had stayed in Virginia something else would've done the job just as good."

"A seed?" I said in a whisper. "What does that mean?"

"It means she inherited this tendency for mental illness, Lyric. It's been there all along just waitin' to hatch. I'll declare I don't know who in the world she got it from."

"Does that mean I got it, too?" I said.

"No, Lyric. The doctor says we're not to worry about you. You know in the past Summer did odd things, but not you. She's always been a little strange."

I nodded. He was right. But nobody had thought she was sick in the head. It was just how she was. We never dreamed she was harboring this seed of mental illness.

"Something was bound to trigger it, the doctor said," Poppy went on. "And adolescence is the usual age for it to go off. It's called schizophrenia."

So now the monster had a name.

We looked at the factory and the icy river shining in the

moonlight. There was an eerie hollowness in the air. Then I was almost sure that I heard a wolf howling. And its lonesomeness went echoing through the frozen streets of Flint. I shivered. I knew it was bound to be my imagination; so why did I glance up at Poppy? If he heard anything, he didn't let on. But he hugged me closer to him.

twelve

I 've found us a house," Poppy said one morning at break-fast. Summer was still in bed. I think it was around the middle of February. He was grinning from ear to ear. "And it's perfect."

"What kind of house?" I said excitedly.

"Two bedrooms, living room, dining room, kitchen, and a bathroom!"

"Hallelujah! Our own bathroom!" I said.

"And a basement, too," he said.

We had never lived in a house with a basement, but it seemed like all the houses in Michigan had one. We couldn't figure out how come.

"Where's it at?" I said.

"Brand Court. It's still in the Zimmerman School dis-trict, so you won't have to change schools."

"Thank Jesus for that."

"It's a short little street out there to itself. It'll be kinda private."

"What about furniture?"

"Well, that's something else. Lucky for us, the people living there now, the Hamiltons—they're friends of Henry's—are moving back to Missouri, and they can't take all their furniture, so they're leaving some of it for us. All I gotta do is take over the payments—about fourteen bucks a month for a bedroom and living-room suite. I think I can get some twin beds real cheap for you and Summer, and a table and four chairs. And guess what? I think I'll buy us a television set!"

"Poppy!" I hollered and clapped my hands together. "A television set!"

"Yeah," Poppy said, looking real satisfied with himself as he started to eat. "We can afford it. You've been good girls, and you deserve a little something extra. I think it'll be good for Summer. It'll occupy her mind."

"I think you're right," I said happily.

And I kissed him on the cheek.

"Wonder what my daddy would think if he could come back and see how well off we're gittin' to be?" Poppy went on.

"I wonder," I said. "He wouldn't know what to think of television, would he, Poppy?"

"I reckon not. He never even heard a radio till he was a great big boy."

For a moment we sat there in silence in our private thoughts. I didn't remember Grandpa. I wondered, if he had not died in that mining accident, would Poppy have left Virginia at all? But then again, maybe Grandpa would've come with us. How nice it would be to have more kin up here in this cold, strange place.

"What about Mama?" I said. "What in the world would she think of Flint, Michigan?"

Poppy smiled and looked away at nothing.

"She was raised in a solitary place, way high on a windy mountaintop," he said. "She told me one time for once in her life she'd like to see something besides hills and sky. So I reckon she'd like it here, Lyric."

And I reckoned she would, too.

The news about the house brightened Summer up considerable. She grew more lively, and her eyes took on some of their old sparkle. She helped me make plans for the new place. Where to put this. Where to put that. What color of curtains to get. Stuff like that.

We moved on a Saturday, and Poppy was supposed to be to work by two o'clock, so we had to get up and do everything before then. Henry helped us with his pickup truck. I don't know what we would've done without Henry. He was real good to us.

After Poppy went to work, the furniture store delivered twin beds for me and Summer, a small dinette set, and the treasured television. But we couldn't watch it yet. There already was an antenna on the top of the house, but we didn't know how to use it. We would have to wait for Henry to hook it up for us.

Summer helped me make the beds, hang up our clothes, and put away things. We worked side by side, sometimes singing in harmony. It was a happy day.

Brand Court was only a few blocks from Glenwood, but

quieter, and less tacky. This was the white house we always dreamed we would live in someday, tiny but tidy, with green shutters and a wrought-iron railing around the porch. It sat at the end of the street against a knoll. There was no front yard, but a small back yard where the Hamiltons had to leave their children's swing set because they hadn't room to haul it back to Missouri.

You went to the basement from the kitchen. And that was something Summer was afraid of. I couldn't get her to go down there even to look at it. She said there were probably wolves hiding under the stairs. But I knew there was nothing but an old wringer washing machine that could still wash clothes pretty good, and shelves against the wall where we could put things we didn't use a lot. After living in two rooms, never had any place seemed so spacious!

The rent was twenty-five dollars a month, which was a bargain. We had furniture in every room, and we had little extra things like hooks in the cabinets to hang up your teacups. In our bedroom me and Summer had new wallpaper with Southern belles on it. They were strolling around under magnolia trees, and carrying tiny umbrellas that matched their dresses.

I remember how we would walk into the bathroom just to look, and to touch the sink maybe. To make sure it was real, I reckon.

We stayed up late to surprise Poppy and he was tickled when he came home from work to find two shining faces and a hot meal waiting for him on our new table. With grateful hearts we sat down and joined hands while

Poppy voiced our thanks to Jesus. Things were looking up.

That night after me and Summer climbed into our twin beds, she said to me, "This feels peculiar, Lyric. It's the first time I can remember that you and me slept in separate beds."

"Want me to come over there with you till you go to sleep?" I said.

"No," she answered after a moment. "I gotta get used to it."

We didn't say anything else. I wondered if her dreams could still get into my head now that we were sleeping apart. I hoped not. I didn't like her dreams.

We had privacy in our new place, just like Poppy had said. None of my classmates from Zimmerman lived on our street, so they wouldn't be seeing Summer and asking me about her. Funny thing about the city. You didn't know what your next-door neighbor was doing, and sometimes you didn't know their names even. Back home, everybody in the county would've known about Summer by now.

Poppy got us a telephone. He told us it didn't have any electricity in it, so Summer wasn't afraid. It was the first one we'd ever had, and I was tickled, but I didn't give anybody at school my number. I was afraid my friends might call and Summer would answer. Then I would have some explainin' to do. Sometimes I wanted to call one of them at night after Summer was in bed, but I had told them we didn't have a phone. So I would just look with yearning at the phone sittin' there silent, and think to myself someday Summer'll be all right again. Someday we'll both be talking on the phone for hours, like normal teenagers do. But for now . . .

One time Gladys said, "Lyric, that first week of school you told me you had a sister at Central High School, but ever since then, you haven't said a thing about her, and when I bring it up, you change the subject. Do you or don't you have a sister?"

We were in the lunchroom, and Yolanda and Nadine were listening. They stopped eating to look at me. They all waited for me to answer.

With my fork I moved the food around on my tray. It was something they called goulash. Hamburger meat and tomatoes in macaroni. Yankee food.

"Yeah, I got a sister," I said softly, without looking up.

"Is she still at Central?" Gladys said.

"No, she had to quit school," I said. "She's been sick."

"I'm so sorry," Nadine said sweetly. "What's wrong with her?"

I didn't know what to say then, so I didn't say anything. Instead, I stuffed my mouth full. They kept on looking at me, then at each other. Drek'ly Gladys and Nadine shrugged and went back to their own goulash. But Yolanda couldn't let a matter drop. She went on with it.

"Well, I want to know what the big mystery is," she said. "What's wrong with her?"

"None of your business!" I said hotly, and that was that. My best friends knew I had a sick sister at home, but that's all they knew. I reckoned nobody else knew anything, and that's how I wanted it.

thirteen

All through March in our snug little house at the end of our private street, me and Summer watched television every free minute. She was afraid to go near it, so I turned it on for her first thing in the morning, and it stayed on till she went to bed at night. We even took our food into the living room, and sat on the sofa and ate. She was enchanted. I guess I was, too.

Every day when I came home from school we watched *Queen for a Day*. It was real good. A bunch of women would get up there and tell their hard-luck stories, and one of them was chosen by the audience to be queen for a day. Then she would get a crown and all kinds of prizes.

We learned to repeat the regular parts right along with Jack Bailey: "Would *you* like to be queen for a day?" And Summer always added, "Yes, I would!"

We also loved *Coke Time* on Wednesday and Friday nights, which starred Eddie Fisher, and *Name That Tune* on Tuesday night. We were real good at naming the tunes.

And on Saturday nights we loved *The Jimmy Durante*

Show. We would both say, "Good night, Mrs. Callabash, wherever you are," right along with Jimmy Durante. He said that at the end of each show as he was walking away under the spotlights.

"Reckon what he means by that?" we wondered out loud. "Reckon who Mrs. Callabash is?"

Then one night Summer said, "It's me."

"You?" I said with a laugh.

"Yeah," she said dreamily. "I'm Mrs. Callabash. It's a secret code for me. Jimmy Durante is talking to me."

"I know you're kidding," I said. "Ain't you?"

"No, I'm not."

"Don't start with that stuff again, Summer," I said crossly.

"What stuff?" she said seriously. "Jimmy Durante is in love with me."

And Summer didn't seem to think that was a weird thing to say.

Another time we were watching Edgar Bergen with his dummies when Summer said, "I think somebody's throwing their voice into my head like that."

"Like what?" I said.

"Like Edgar Bergen does with his dolls, Charlie McCarthy and Mortimer Snerd. Know what I mean? It's called ventriloquism."

I knew about the voices, but she had never called it ventriloquism before.

"That's it," she said softly. "Somebody's throwing voices into my head."

"And what do they say?"

"All kinds of things. They say all kinds of things to me, and I can't make them hush."

Another show we liked was *The Perry Como Show*. One night me and Poppy were awakened around 4 a.m. by Summer singing. Her voice sounded so beautiful that night, it was downright unearthly. She was out there on the swing set in the back yard in her nightgown, just swingin' and singin' Perry Como's theme song.

> *Dream along with me*
> *I'm on my way to the stars*
> *Come along, come along*
> *Leave your worries far behind!*

We went out and got her and led her back into the house. Her skin was like ice, but she didn't seem to be cold. She went on singing. She was also laughing a real funny laugh that didn't come from her heart at all, just from her throat.

The next morning I asked her, "Why did you do such a thing?"

"They told me to do it," she replied.

"Who told you?"

"The voices."

"They told you to go outside in the cold with nothing on your arms and feet?"

"Yeah, it was the President. He has appointed me to investigate Communism."

"And that's why you were out there?"

"See, it's Mamie Eisenhower's birthday, and Jimmy Durante couldn't go," she went on.

"Summer, talk sense to me!" I said, stomping my foot in total exasperation.

"They told me to," she said lamely, then she added, "Jibble, jibble, groggle . . ."

"Groggle" was a new word she had invented. It made perfect sense to her.

That day Poppy called the doctor, and he upped the dosage of Summer's medication.

"Doctor says the day is coming when pills won't control her behavior," Poppy whispered to me. "Her body develops a tolerance to them, see? And after a while they'll have no effect on her."

"What will we do then, Poppy?"

"I don't know. I just don't know. Doctor says we might have to commit her."

"Commit her to what?"

"To the asylum in Pony-ac, Lyric," he said sadly.

He meant Pontiac. Everybody back home said *Pony-ac*, but it was one of those words I had learned to say right at school.

"Oh, no, Poppy, not a lunatic asylum!"

"Listen, Lyric, even with my good insurance from GM, the medical bills are awful. I can't begin to pay for all the treatment she needs. I can't even pronounce or halfway understand all the things they want to do for her. But Doctor says if I put her in Pony-ac, I can make her a ward of the State of Michigan, and they'll take care of her. They'll know what to do for her. They can give her the very best of care for free."

"If she's made a ward of the state, will they ever give her back to us?" I said.

"I reckon so, when she gets better," Poppy said, "they'll give her back. Yeah, they'll give her back."

"But will she get better?"

"I just don't know," Poppy said wearily. "The only thing I know for sure is that she needs a lot more help than she's gettin' now."

"But in the asylum she won't have us, Poppy," I said. "Summer has never been away from us."

"I know," Poppy said. "We won't do anything a'tall yet, Lyric. We'll take it one day at a time."

He paused and repeated, "We'll take it one day at a time."

fourteen

My fourteenth birthday fell on the last Saturday in March that year. It seemed funny to look outside and see traces of snow. And the ground was still half-frozen. Back home in Virginia the crocuses would be pushing up through the soft black dirt, and the buttercups would be in bloom.

But back home I wouldn't be studying music in school. Yolanda, Nadine, and Gladys wouldn't be there either. Poppy wouldn't be able to afford a television and a telephone. And he couldn't give me ten dollars and tell me to go shopping for my birthday, which is what he did!

"Ten whole dollars?" I said. "You mean it, Poppy?"

"Sure I mean it. You didn't have much of a Christmas. Buy yourself something pretty."

Summer heard that, and I was surprised when she said she wanted to go shopping with me.

So I told her, "Summer, I want you to go with me, but you have to promise not to act up."

"I won't," she said weakly.

"We can spend the whole day down on Saginaw Street like we did when we first came to Flint, 'member?"

"Yeah," she said, smiling. "Can we buy something good to eat?"

"Sure."

At school I'd been hearing about this place downtown called Kewpie's where they sold hamburgers and hot dogs, and they said if you wanted to meet cute boys, Kewpie's was the place to go. But I was afraid we might run into somebody I knew there.

Then I realized I was doing it again. I was trying to hide Summer, and I couldn't do that forever. Besides, she had seemed better since the doctor increased her medication, so I decided to take a chance and tell her about Kewpie's.

"Goody! I'd like to meet me some cute boys," she said with a giggle. "Let's eat lunch there."

We dressed up in our black slacks which everybody called slim-jims that year, and oversized white shirts, and we decided not to wear boots. It was warm enough to wear our penny loafers and bobby socks. Boots didn't look good with slim-jims.

I helped Summer cut and clean her fingernails, and polish them. Her hands looked very nice then, and her hair had grown out to its usual length. We tucked it back behind her ears, and clipped it there with silver hair bows.

Then we both put on our light jackets instead of overcoats, and headed out to the bus stop, as giddy as we'd been the week of the Centennial. That seemed like a long time ago.

At Kresge's I picked out some Precious Pink lipstick to match the nail polish we were both wearing, which I had bought Summer for her birthday. I got some other stuff too, and when I realized half of my money was spent, we left the dime store before it all disappeared, and went window shopping.

Though the air was chilly, the sun was shining bright, and the sky was perfectly blue, about the color of Summer's eyes, so I told her that. She smiled and hooked her arm through mine.

"Your eyes are that blue, too!" she said. "You are lookin' so grownup these days, Lyric, and so cute."

"Ree . . . al . . . lee?"

To get a compliment from Summer was special, because I knew she was always honest with me. I could trust her opinion.

"Yeah," she said. "You're real pretty."

I wisht then I could say the same thing about her. But the madness and medication had taken its toll on her appearance.

Before I could think of something nice to say, Summer said, "My looks don't matter to me anymore."

It was like she had read my mind. "When a person is like me, your worries are more important than anything else. I usta get all tangled up in my mind. But lately I've been thinking clear, and I've been given sacred visions. I see all the millions—I reckon even billions—of people who lived on this earth before us, and . . ."

"Don't start, Summer," I pleaded.

"No, I'm serious now," she said and began to talk real fast. She was trying to get everything out before her train of thought derailed. That was apt to happen to her sometimes.

"A hundred years ago there was a girl who was as troubled as me . . . and the world revolved around her worries, at least in her mind it did . . . but today she lays buried in a grave . . . and nobody knows what happened to her . . . or remembers her name or anything about her . . . she's forgotten, Lyric . . . *forgotten* . . . and the world goes on without her, on and on, turning around and around . . . and other girls have walked the earth . . . boys, too . . . millions of 'em . . . each one growing up laughing and dancing and having sweethearts . . . and thinking they're the only one who ever felt this way . . . the only one who ever had troubles . . . then they are lost and forgotten . . ."

"What makes you think of things like that?" I said.

"I don't know. I just think. I think all the time. And voices come to me and tell me things. A hundred years from now—in the year 2056—I'll be in a grave, and another girl will be wondering . . ."

Summer stopped abruptly to look at some books that were on display in the window of a bookstore. There was one on ghosts. Summer pointed to it and said, "That's what ghosts are, you know. They are people like me from long ago. And they're still wandering the earth, all caught up in their earthly problems and they can't give it up."

"Summer, you said you wouldn't do this."

"I know," she said, and we continued walking down the street. "I just wisht I knew how to keep from fading away."

"Try not to think about it."

But there was no shutting her up.

"Out of all those millions, only a handful are remembered," she went on sadly. "Sometimes in books they are kept alive."

We walked along in silence for a minute.

Then, "Will you write a book about me, Lyric?"

"Sure I will. Now hush up!" She was getting on my nerves.

"Promise?"

"I promise!" I said irritably. "Let's go eat lunch."

So we went to Kewpie's. Lots of other teenagers were there, but nobody I knew. I was relieved. There were three cute boys in the next booth, and they smiled at us.

After a while one of the boys said, "Hey, you," and we turned around to talk to him.

"What's your name?"

"Lyric," I said.

"Summer," she said.

"Where do you go to school?"

"Zimmerman," I said, and Summer didn't say anything.

"Oh, I know some kids from Zimmerman. Do you know . . . ?"

He started naming people, and some of them I knew and some of them I didn't. We got to talking, and the other two boys joined in. They said their names were Larry, Curly, and Moe, but I knew better. I said they just *acted* like Larry, Curly, and Moe. Then they laughed and gave me their real names—Steve, Michael, and Mark, Michigan names.

"We met each other through the busy line," Steve said.

"The what?"

"Don't you know about the busy line?" Mark said.

"No, what is it?"

"It's a telephone number you can dial," Mark explained. "And you always get a busy signal—always. But if you listen hard, over the signal you can hear other kids yelling."

"Yelling?" I said.

"Yeah, they'll be yelling their telephone numbers," Michael joined in.

I smiled at him. He was the cutest one. He was my pick.

"And you can hear the numbers over the busy signal?" I said.

I didn't know much about telephones, but that seemed peculiar to me. How could it be?

"Yeah," Michael went on. "I don't know how it happens, but you can hear."

"So everybody yells their phone numbers into this line," Steve went on, "and if you listen, you can zero in on a particular voice. So you call the number the voice is yelling, and that's how lots of kids get to know each other."

"That's right—through the busy line," Michael finished. "And here's the number. Try it."

He handed me a little piece of napkin with a phone number on it.

It was then I realized that nobody was talking to Summer. The boys were saying all this stuff to me. They were ignoring her, and she had gone quiet. I was trying to figure out how to draw her into the conversation when she excused herself to go to the rest room.

I went right on talking and joking with the boys until Summer got back. Then I saw that she had taken my Precious Pink lipstick and tried to put it on her lips, but she had missed. It was all over the place, up above and below her mouth, but she seemed to be real pleased with herself. She was grinning this big grin, and I could see she had lipstick on her teeth, too. She looked absolutely grotesque.

And for one awful second I saw the face of crazy Sadie where my sister's face shoulda been.

"Look what you've done," I said to her with an embarrassed laugh, "you've smeared your lipstick."

The boys got quiet as they stared at her, and I felt my face turn red. All the other kids there were sniggering and pointing at her.

"Go back in there and fix it," I whispered to her.

She stopped grinning and, without a word, got up and returned to the rest room. I didn't feel like talking and joking around anymore, so I said nothing else to the boys. I didn't even look up as I took money out of my purse and started to the cash register to pay.

"What's wrong with your mom?" Mark said to me as I went by the boys' table.

"My mom?" I stopped in my tracks and faced him just in time to see Michael elbow him in the ribs.

"Yeah, ain't that woman your mom?"

I didn't answer him. I went on my way and paid the cashier; then I stood by the door to wait for Summer to come out of the rest room. I felt so bad I wanted to go on home and forget about spending the rest of my birthday money.

After a while Michael came to me and said, "Hey, if you're waiting for that woman, she went out the other door."

"What!"

"Yeah, she went out that side door while you were paying."

I hurried out the door he pointed to and looked up and down the street, but Summer was nowhere to be seen. Then I went back inside and double-checked the rest room. No Summer. I ran through Kewpie's to the outside again. All the kids were watching me now, but I was hardly aware of them. This was no time to be embarrassed. I was scared.

Breathlessly, I went back in and said to Michael, "Did you see which way she went?"

"No, I just saw her go out the door," he said. "Sorry. What's wrong with her?"

"She's sick," I said. I was practically wringing my hands. "She shouldn't be alone."

"I'll help you look for her," he said kindly as he climbed out of the booth.

Together me and Michael walked up and down the street real fast, looking everywhere. No luck. Then we walked slowly back to Kewpie's.

There was nothing left but to call Poppy at work. I had never had to do that before, but his number was in my purse. He had given it to me for emergencies, and I reckoned this was one. There was a phone booth on the street corner.

"Stay right where you are!" Poppy said to me. "I'll be there soon's I can get away."

I hung up, turned to Michael, and said, "Thanks for your help. There's nothing else you can do."

"You sure?" he said. Later I remembered how good-hearted he had been.

"I'm sure. You can go on back to your friends."

At least I think that's what I said. My thoughts were racing. What to do? What to do? Oh, Summer, why did you do this? Were your feelings hurt to be left out? Or didn't you know what you were doing? Where is your poor little mind taking you to?

I sat on a bench at the bus stop in front of the restaurant, waiting for Poppy. Pretty soon Michael, Mark, and Steve came out the door and saw me. They all stopped to tell me goodbye, and said they hoped Summer would be all right.

I said something to them. I don't know what.

"Be sure to call the busy line when you get a chance," Michael said. "I think you'll find it interesting."

"Yeah, thanks," I mumbled.

fifteen

oppy got there on a bus in about half an hour, and we started walking up and down the street together, asking people in the business places if they had seen Summer. We described her as best we could, knowing that once a person saw that haunted face, they were not likely to forget it. But nobody could recall seeing her.

"At that bus stop," Poppy said to me. "Do you think she might've caught a bus?"

"I don't know if she had any money with her. Do you know?"

"No," Poppy said. "She ain't asked me for money in a long time. She never went anywheres."

Then he let out one of those long, heavy sighs. "I think there's nothing left to do but call the police."

I reckoned he was right. So we called the police, and they came, and they went through a long list of questions for us. They asked for a picture, and Poppy had one in his billfold, but it was of that beautiful Summer in our memories who didn't much resemble the sick Summer. I knew that's why Poppy had not shown it to the people in the business places.

Poppy told the policemen how bad off she was, and they could see how worried we were. They patted Poppy on the back and me on the head and told us to go on home now and try not to worry. They would call us in a while.

So we did go home, and all through the rest of the afternoon we paced the floor. Ever' now and then we peered out the window. We sat down at the eating table once or twice and nibbled on some leftovers. We watched the phone and willed it to ring. But we never talked about Summer, or about anything else. We had run out of things to say. Still, I knew all the while Poppy's mind was going a hundred miles an hour, like mine was . . . wondering, worrying . . .

She didn't have on her boots, and it was getting colder outside as the day fell into evening. She didn't have on her winter coat either.

What could she be thinking? Did she remember what Poppy had said that time about bad things happening to young girls in big cities? Did she remember our telephone number? Did she know how to call from a public phone? She must be so scared!

I didn't know how many practical things she remembered. Did she even know her address? Why, oh why didn't we go over these things with her?

Ring, phone, ring . . .

I recalled another spring day back in the hills when me and Summer went to visit Aunt June without Poppy's permission. We were only six and nine then, I think. And we had walked all by ourselves down to the highway, playing and picking violets along the way, while Poppy was worried sick. Now I knew how he had felt.

We heard a car door slam and hurried to the window. There was a man opening the passenger door of a Buick, and someone was getting out. The man was Bill from Glenwood Avenue, and the someone was Summer!

We rushed outside. I went to Summer, and Poppy grabbed Bill up off of the ground by his collar and pushed him against the car real rough. I thought he was bound to kill the poor man.

"What were you doing with my girl!" he hollered right in Bill's face.

Bill turned red, and his eyes looked like they were gonna pop out of his head.

"What's the matter with Poppy?" Summer whispered frantically to me.

"Whadda *you* think?" I snapped. "He was worried to death!"

"Did you hurt her?" Poppy said to Bill through clenched teeth.

"I sw . . . swear to God, Mr. C . . . Compton," Bill stammered. "I ain't t . . . touched her. She come to Glenwood. She said she walked from downtown. And she ast me to take her to a pi'ture show. But I wouldn't do it. I talked her into coming home. And I brung her here. I swear to God that's all there was to it. I swear."

Poppy seemed unsure of what to do next. Slowly he let

go of Bill. Summer started humming to herself and looking up at the sky, like she saw a vision up there. It was another of those peculiar things she used to do as a little girl when she didn't want to see what was happening in the real world. But I hadn't seen her do it in a long time.

"I know she's mental," Bill said real low, but I still heard him. Then he rubbed his neck where Poppy had grabbed him. "I wouldn't hurt her, Mr. Compton."

"All right," Poppy mumbled. "All right."

Then he took Summer by the arm and hauled her into the house. He was upset. He didn't know how to act.

Me and Bill were left standing there looking at each other.

"Thanks," I mumbled, "for bringing her home."

He straightened himself up, and said crossly, "She's been calling me a lot."

"She don't know what she's doin'," I said. "She's sick."

"Well, can you git her to stop?"

"I'll try."

And with that Bill got back in his car and drove away real quick. I went into the house. Summer had gone to our room while Poppy was on the phone with the police. When I went in there, she was sitting on the edge of the bed, still humming, and smiling a silly smile.

I sat down beside her on the bed. "Summer, why did you run away from me like that?"

"Bill's in love with me," she said.

Then I lost it. "Why are you acting so ugly? He said

you've been calling him, and he wants you to stop! Why don't you straighten up? Do you want to go to the asylum? Do you?"

"What do you mean, Lyric?" she said in a hoarse whisper.

"Nothing."

"What did you mean by that?"

I could feel her trembling, and her hands started fluttering.

"I didn't mean anything," I said. "I was foolin'."

"Is Poppy gonna put me in a *place*?"

" 'Course not!"

But she knew I was lying to her. I had lost my temper and what good had it done? Now she had something else to be afraid of.

Then, just like that, I saw Summer's face go totally blank. It was uncanny and unnatural. That's what it was. And I could tell by her lack of expression that nobody was home in there. Summer had retreated to a safe place deep inside where nothing or nobody could touch her.

"Try to get her to take a bath, why don'cha, Lyric?" Poppy said to me as he was going out the door to work the next Saturday.

For the entire week Summer had not reappeared. Only her body was there and it would not bathe or dress or comb its hair. It stunk, and it stayed in bed most all the time, staring at the ceiling.

"I'll try, Poppy."

But when I suggested a bath, Summer said in her tiny voice, "I can't. Water washes me away."

"No, no, Summer," I said. "That's silly. Water does not wash you away."

Finally, I managed to coax her into the bathroom by telling her that Poppy wanted his little girls to be squeaky clean. That took us both back to our childhood in Glory Bottom when we were waiting for Poppy to come home from the mines and spend some time with us.

"Sometimes I miss the hills," she said softly, and I knew her wandering mind had returned, but I didn't know for how long.

I helped her ease into the tub of hot, soapy water, and I washed her hair. Then I sat on the john and talked to her while she relaxed in the suds.

"Would you like to go back home?" I asked her.

"No!" she came back in a flash. "If you look at the world as a house, Lyric, Glory Bottom is the crawl space."

I laughed a genuine laugh then. Yeah, I reckoned the real Summer had made a brief visit. Always the clever one. And she smiled a genuine smile.

Later I helped her dry and wrap herself up in a robe. As she wiped the steam away from the mirror over the sink I came up behind her and our eyes met in the reflection.

"See, Lyric? I'm fading away," she said softly. "See? I'm almost gone."

sixteen

here were things about living in the hills that I didn't miss a bit. Like kids coming to school with lice, or smelling like pee. Wormy kids. Kids with crusty elbows and knees 'cause they had no soap or running water in their houses. Things like the stink of the slate dumps. Coal trucks lumbering over the dirt roads, trailing black dust to coat everything in their wake. Outhouses and shacks hanging off the hillsides.

You didn't see things like that in the city of Flint. But you didn't see spring coming to life either, at least not the way I remembered it. Take the emerald green of the hills. So brilliant it hurt your eyes.

But maybe it wasn't that radiant at all, I thought. Maybe I dreamed it. Lots of times, things are not really as good as you remember them later. On the other hand, some stuff has a tendency to fade, like the faces of my kinfolks. We had been gone only seven months, and I found them hard to recollect. And what about my former classmates? I had forgotten some of their names!

This is how we let things slip away, I told myself. We get all involved in other things, allowing the present to fade into the past.

> *. . . summer turns to winter*
> *and the present disappears.*

In my new life I was falling in love with Gilbert and Sullivan's *The Mikado*, which the combined music classes at Zimmerman were fixin' to produce. You wouldn't never find something like this back home. And you wouldn't find wonderful music teachers like Mrs. Gaspar and Mr. German either.

We did a lot of singing in Mrs. Gaspar's music class, and my friends were always saying, "Wow, Lyric, you're really good!" It made me proud. I only wisht they could hear me and Summer harmonize together, but I didn't mention it.

They told me I had a chance for a part in *The Mikado*, not just in the chorus, but a good part like Pitti-Sing or Peep-Bo. I didn't dare hope for Yum-Yum. Everybody said Yum-Yum would be a ninth-grader. I was so excited I learned all the lyrics to all the songs. I went around humming "Three Little Maids from School Are We," until Poppy started humming it, too. He laughed when I told him what he was singing.

"Tell me about this play," he said to me. "Will I get to see it?"

"Sure, if you want to," I said, but already I was wondering what we would do with Summer while Poppy came to the play. To take her along was out of the question. She had started making funny whistling noises, and she couldn't keep her mind on anything, not even her favorite television shows anymore. Sometimes she'd jump up and start pacing and jabbering right in the middle of one. I could imagine her doing that during *The Mikado*.

It was three weeks into April when I had to stay after school for the tryouts. By then it didn't get dark so early, and I wasn't worried about getting home to Summer. I told her I was going to try out for a part in an operetta and I would be late coming home, but she wasn't listening. At least I thought she wasn't. She was sitting there on the edge of her bed, rocking and shaking her leg. Her doctor called what she was doing perseverating. He said it was a common thing for a mentally ill person to do. She was also making that funny noise.

"I'll be ri'cheer with her till two o'clock," Poppy reassured me. "I'll give her something t'eat before I go to work, and she'll be O.K. till you come home."

Nearabout half of the kids at Zimmerman showed up in the auditorium for the tryouts after school. Mr. German and Mrs. Gaspar were sitting at the piano deciding how they were gonna do stuff, while everybody else was milling around, talking and making noise. So I went off into a corner by myself and started going over Pitti-Sing's part.

I was mouthing the words low to myself when I became aware that something was going on about halfway back in the auditorium. I didn't want to be distracted right then, so I closed my eyes and concentrated harder.

Then a hush fell, and I heard a familiar, "Jibble . . . jibble . . ."

Lordy mercy, don't let that mean what I think it means!

Slowly I turned my head to where my classmates had congregated. I could see only the backs of young people crowded around something, but I *knew* what was at the center of their attention. I walked over there and eased myself far enough amongst them that I could see.

Summer was sitting there at the end of one of the rows of seats shaking her leg furiously and making that funny blowing sound with her mouth. She was real agitated. Her eyes were darting rapidly from place to place, settling on nothing.

I realized in that moment what Yolanda had meant when she had said, "They'll peck you to death if you're different."

Peck! Peck!

"Look at that funny woman!"

"Jibble, jibble," Summer said, and my classmates burst into laughter.

Peck! Peck!

"Hey, crater face!"

Peck! Peck!

"Where's your shoes at, looney?"

"Groggle."

"Did you say, 'Gobble, gobble?'"

More laughter.

My darkest emotions surfaced.

First shame.

There was simply no keeping this skeleton in the closet. It was obvious she *had* heard me that morning, and she had come to see the tryouts.

Then anger.

How come she could understand only what she wanted to understand? How come she pretended she wasn't listening to me? Why was she playing games with me?

And grief.

Oh, Mama, Mama, I miss you so! Why did you have to die and leave me all alone like this?

Of all the things that might have come into my mind right then, why did I think of that? Why should I suddenly long for my mother with all my heart and soul when I had never felt that way before?

Then a jumbled collage of the past and present played out before me like one of Summer's ghostly hallucinations.

I see that she is wearing her house slippers . . . and I remember Summer teaching me how to tie my shoe strings.

I hear her making that sound with her mouth . . . and I remember Summer teaching me to whistle.

Her dress is on backwards . . . and I remember Summer washing a stain out of my favorite dress on a Saturday night so I can wear it to Sunday School the next morning.

Her hair needs combing . . . and I remember Summer gently brushing the tangles out of my baby-fine hair.

A thousand acts of love . . . saving her singing money to buy me a present . . . kissing away my tears . . .

"Gobble, gobble!" Dewey the heckler mocks her . . . and I remember Summer rescuing me from bullies at school.

I pushed my way through the kids and gave Dewey a shove that sent him sprawling into the crowd. He yelped. Somebody caught him and kept him on his feet.

I went to my sister's side. "It's O.K., Summer," I said. "I'm here."

She jumped out of her seat, grabbed my arm, and clung to it. Everybody got quiet then. They were all staring with their mouths open. They were wondering if Lyric Compton knew this funny-lookin' person. Maybe they were wondering if we were kin. And they couldn't wait to find out!

"Jibble, jibble, groggle . . ." Summer said. She wanted to tell me something, but the right words were lost to her.

Whisperings rippled through the group like a breeze through leaves. I saw my three best friends standing there together gaping.

"This is my sister, Summer," I said directly to Yolanda, Nadine, and Gladys.

I said it clearly and dramatically, just as I had rehearsed saying, "I am Pitti-Sing, sister to Yum-Yum."

Some kids sniggered, but my friends looked upon us kindly.

At that moment Summer tugged at my sleeve excitedly and said, "Lyric, am I queen for a day?"

Then she covered her face with her hands as the auditorium exploded with laughter. You couldn't much blame them, I thought. Maybe it was kinda funny. But it didn't feel funny to me. I was afraid that I might cry. I could feel the hot angry tears just ready to boil over, but I wouldn't let them.

"What's going on?" I heard as Mrs. Gaspar and Mr. German stepped into the circle and saw me there with Summer.

"My sister's sick," I said quietly. "I'll be taking her home now."

On the way home Summer said to me, "I didn't know where you were at, Lyric, and I needed you. There was a goblin. He was 'lectric . . . a little 'lectric goblin, and I was afraid of him . . . the F.B.I. sent him to spy on me."

I was thinking that night that it was getting harder and harder to love Summer, and to forgive her for her weirdness. When I discovered that thought in my head, I felt so guilty I went into the bedroom where she was supposed to be sleeping to check on her and give her a hug.

There she was sitting in the middle of the bed playing with matches. She was striking one after another and throwing them, lit, onto the floor, where they burnt little brown spots into the linoleum.

I had to fight Summer to get the matches away from her, but I finally did it, and I hid all the others that I could find in the house. The next day she lit a candle from the flame on the gas stove. Poppy found out when he saw that the stove was on, and when he went in to ask Summer about it, she was burning a candle right beside her curtains.

So now we had something else to be afraid of. We couldn't let her out of our sight.

seventeen

On a Friday evening in May I went to see *The Mikado* by myself. I mouthed all the words as they were sung onstage, and my heart hurt because I felt so left out.

It was Poppy's night off, so he stayed home with Summer. He had coaxed it out of me what had happened at the tryouts, and I could see the sadness in his eyes. In fact, he felt so bad he said he was going to hire somebody to look after Summer whenever I wanted some time to go do things like that by myself and he had to work.

"I don't want you to be embarrassed, and to be left out of things on account of her," he told me. " 'Cause then you'll start resenting your sister, and I won't let that happen."

But I didn't want to blame anything on Summer. I knew she couldn't help it. She was my sister, for crying out loud! She just couldn't help how she was. Still, it would be nice not to have to worry about her when I had something to do.

So Poppy started looking for somebody suitable to come

in for a few hours once in a while. And he found Beatrice, who was the daughter of a West Virginia feller Poppy worked with.

Bea, as everybody called her, was eighteen and done with school. She had been in Flint for two years, so her accent was mongrel. She had a boyfriend by the name of Roy Rivers, who had adopted a lot of Bea's expressions and ways because he thought they were cute, but I had learned to recognize the real thoroughbred Yankees, no matter how they acted. They always gave themselves away in little ways, like the so-called country singer on television who called a fiddle a violin.

Bea and Roy came over one Sunday evening to meet Summer, but she was sullen with them and wouldn't raise her eyes to meet theirs. She went on watching the television and wouldn't let me turn it off. Still, Bea talked to her in loud, careful words, like Summer was hard of hearing.

"Summer," Bea said, laying one hand on her arm. *"Roy and I would love to visit with you once in a while. Is that all right with you?"*

At which Summer irritably shook off Bea's hand, and didn't even answer.

"Well, that's O.K.," Bea whispered to me and Poppy. "When it comes to making friends, me and Roy never met a nut we couldn't crack, did we, Roy?"

And she turned to Roy and punched him playfully with her elbow. They both giggled. They were always giggling. But I didn't think that was so funny.

I figure about that time it dawned on Bea what she had said, 'cause she turned red.

She tried to explain, "I didn't mean anything. I meant me and Roy never met a stranger. We're just so full of ourselves, people get tickled at us all the time."

"Right!" Roy said. "That Bea's crazy as they come."

That Roy shoulda kept his mouth shut. Now they were both blushing.

Poppy explained as best he could what Summer's sickness was like, how she was liable to hurt herself or set the house on fire, and what they would be expected to do when they stayed with her, mainly just watch her close.

"We can handle that," Bea and Roy both said, and giggled again.

"It was very nice to meet you, Summer," Bea said carefully as she was leaving, but Summer ignored her.

When they were gone, me and Poppy looked at each other, wondering if we could really trust that silly couple with our Summer. But we reckoned we'd give them a chance.

When school let out at the end of May, I called the number of the busy line which Michael had given me that day at Kewpie's. Funny thing, it wasn't busy. In fact, it was Michael who answered!

"You were foolin' me!" I said with a laugh. "There's no such thing as the busy line!"

"Yeah, there really is," Michael said. "That was the

truth, and I'll give you the real number if you'd like it. But I wanted you to call me."

And that was the beginning of my friendship with Michael Beaver. We talked on the phone a lot, and Poppy let us meet for lunch at Kewpie's of a Saturday, and he would let Michael come to the house when he was there too, but he wouldn't let me go on a date yet.

With me out of school, we found that we didn't have to call on Bea to come sit with Summer. I could do lots of things I wanted to do before Poppy went to work at 2 p.m., and he was off two nights a week to look after her. But on the nights he had to work, I stayed home.

Sometimes I had a chance to go picnicking, swimming, roller skating, bowling, or to ball games and movies with my friends. There were lots of things to do in Michigan, and I took advantage of them when Poppy was at home with Summer.

Gayle Stiltner introduced us to her church, and we liked it. Lots of Southern people went there, and we started going every Sunday. Poppy went to the 9 a.m. service and I went at eleven.

About that time I discovered a sneaky streak in that mixed-up mind of Summer's. For example, she'd pretend to be just sitting and staring out the window until she thought you were not paying her any attention. Then she would very quietly go rummaging around for something to stick in the flames on the gas stove.

When I figured out what she was doing, she would run

out the door and down the street. Then I had to go chasing after her, and yelling for her through the neighborhood. She would go into people's yards and hide in the bushes or around behind the garages. When I gave up on finding her and went back home, there she was, messing around with fire again! It like to scared me witless. I caught on to that trick after the second time, luckily before she burnt the house down.

Then she took up another dangerous thing—playing with sharp things. One day I found her cutting her fingernails with a razor blade, and blood was dripping all over her housecoat. I was horrified. It made me hurt just to look at her poor hands.

That doubled our worries 'cause now we had to keep anything sharp out of her reach, and matches, too. She was still afraid to go down into the basement, so I could hide stuff from her there. Poppy took to carrying his razor blades to work with him so I wouldn't have to worry about them.

But when she wasn't mutilating herself or playing with fire, Summer was sitting quiet and doing nothing. It was easy enough to forget that she could be dangerous.

Poppy bought a picnic table for the back yard so we could eat out there in warm weather. It was a Michigan thing to do, and lots of fun. One weekend when he was off, he invited Gayle, her son, Paul, and Paul's girlfriend, Lily, over for hamburgers. He also invited Henry and his new girlfriend, Wilma Dean.

The next time, he let me invite Michael, Gladys, Nadine, Yolanda, and Yolanda's friend, Ike. That lil' ole house had never heard so much laughter! We ate out in our private back yard, and just had the best time.

I thought of how I had dreaded for other people to see Summer, because I was ashamed. But now I learned that the most important people—at least to me and Poppy— were kind. In fact, I had greatly underestimated my friends.

We all went out of our way to include Summer in our picnics, but she did not like having other people around her. In fact, she hated it, and she angrily retreated to our bedroom and slammed the door. And if me or Poppy took her something to eat and begged her to come out, she would just shout at us to go away.

"Give her time to get used to you," Poppy would say to our guests. "She'll get over it."

But she never did.

At these times when we had company, the hardest part was making Summer clean herself up before they got there. First I would go into the bathroom, run the water, and get everything ready. Then Poppy would grab Summer and force her into the bathroom. Once he had in her there, he would stand outside the door and wouldn't let her out until she had bathed, washed her hair, and put on clean clothes. And I was in there with her to make sure she did it. Oh, it made her so mad! She would cuss and cry and holler the whole time. But she would finally do what she was told, just to get out of the bathroom.

Wildflowers managed to find a place to grow out on that little knoll behind our house. One time when I looked out there I was reminded again of home. How the katydids would be doing their summer songs. How the creeks and the river would be sparkling in the afternoon sunshine. The smell of summer rain. The sky a channel of blue you had to look straight up to see. The children roaming the hills, climbing trees. Bluebells and wild pink roses. Swimming holes. Ball games in the road.

But now those images appeared in my head like a movie I had once seen that had nothing to do with me. How strange, I thought, my far home is now like a place I've only seen pictures of.

But most of the time I was too busy to remember even the pictures. I had a new home, a new life, far removed from Glory Bottom. By the time the changeover came at General Motors, we had forgotten our plans to go back to the hills for a visit. Our new life had usurped the old one.

eighteen

One Saturday in the middle of July I was invited to go with Gladys and her daddy, her brother and her brother's friend to Detroit and see the Detroit Tigers play baseball. We would be gone all day. Poppy had to work, but he said this was a chance I must not throw away, so he called Bea to come stay with Summer.

And that was the day that Summer managed to sneak matches out of one of Poppy's shirt pockets. Only it wasn't the curtains or the house she wanted to burn that day—it was herself.

"We missed her for a few minutes," Bea told me later, "and when we went into the bedroom to find her, there she was sitting in the middle of the bed holding a flaming match to her arm. It was burning the flesh of her arm at one end and her fingers at the other end. And she didn't even say 'ouch!'"

Bea had gone into a screaming fit while Roy took the matches away from Summer. She had five big ugly burned places on her left arm. Roy called Poppy at work, and he came home and took Summer to the emergency room, where they put her in the psychiatric ward again.

A new young intern cared for her this time. His name was Dr. Elliott, and he took a special interest in Summer's case.

"This child needs to be in the hospital at Pontiac," he told Poppy.

"I don't want to just lock her up," Poppy said.

"It's not a prison," the doctor said kindly. "You can take her home for holidays and vacations. And if she gets well, they'll release her. It's important for schizophrenics to know that the family still cares about them, but Summer needs medications and special treatments that you can't give her at home."

"Well, I reckon I'll consider it when school starts again," Poppy told the young doctor.

"School?" Dr. Elliott said, not understanding.

"Yeah, my other girl, Lyric, she's fourteen, and she does a real good job with Summer, but she'll be going into the ninth grade in September, and . . ."

"A fourteen-year-old girl is not capable . . . She should not even be left alone with Summer," Dr. Elliott said firmly.

Which gave Poppy something else to worry about.

"Dr. Elliott thinks taking care of Summer is too hard on you, Lyric, and too dangerous for both of you," he said to me that night. "And he could be right. Maybe it's time to, you know . . ."

"Poppy, no!" I said. "We can't just throw her out—*throw her to the wolves*!"

"I don't know what else to do, Lyric," he said. "I'll declare I don't."

"Let's try another sitter, maybe an older person this time," I suggested. "There must be somebody we can trust to stay with her just that short period, from the time you go to work until I get home from school, and maybe some evenings, too, when I have to go somewhere."

"All right," Poppy agreed. "We'll give it another shot."

When Summer returned from the hospital, she was all drugged up again, but this time the medication wore off real fast and she came out of it mad at the world.

We hired a woman named Susie to come stay with Summer for one evening. I went over to Nadine's house for a couple of hours just to see how Susie and Summer would get along. But Summer sneaked away, and we had to call the police again. She wasn't found until the next morning, when a neighbor spotted her asleep behind a bush in her yard.

Then came Margie. Summer hit her and broke her glasses. Lucy followed, and Summer cussed her out. Myrtle was locked out of the house, and Ginger was burned while trying to put out a fire . . .

One balmy afternoon in August, Poppy was at work and Summer was asleep when I first became aware of this eerie stillness in the air. I walked out on our tiny back porch to see if I could figure out what was amiss. I found myself looking up into a gray cover that reminded me of the troubled sky in the wolf nightmare—dark, turbulent, rolling.

The telephone rang, and I ran back inside to answer the ring before it woke Summer up. It was Poppy.

"Lyric," he said. "You got the television on?"

"No," I said. "Why?"

"Well, turn it on. I hear they got tornado warnings. I don't believe y'all are in the danger zone, but just the same, you watch and listen."

"Tornado warnings?" I said. "Ree . . . al . . . lee?" I thought that was exciting news, something to write home about.

"Yeah, if there comes a tornado, you follow instructions, you heah me? You do what they tell you on the television."

I turned on the TV just as a man was saying that a close tornado sounds like a train is coming into the house, and if you should happen to hear that noise, you better get yourself down in the basement fast. And that's when I figured out why Michigan houses have basements.

I heard Summer get up and go to the refrigerator. I could smell her before she entered the living room. She was drinking Kool-Aid from a coffee cup, and she looked awful. Her face was puffy from sleep, her hair filthy, and she was wearing the same shorty pajamas she had been wearing for the last four or five days. I had tried to get them off of her once, but she had fought me away.

"I'll change clothes when I get damn good and ready!" she had said hotly. "So mind your own beeswax!"

That's how she was now. Sometimes she even called me

nasty names. I mean *real* nasty. She said words that Poppy used to spank us both for saying. But nowadays he would look the other way with sad, lost eyes. He didn't know what to do.

"I wanna see Art Linkletter," Summer said.

"He's not on," I said. "There's tornado warnings. Poppy said for us to watch."

"Where's Art Linkletter?" She raised her voice.

"He's not on!" I snapped and turned up the volume so I could hear what the weatherman was saying.

"He's always on at this time!" Summer screamed. "Who's that man yonder?"

"He's talking about tornadoes," I said. "We have to listen to him."

"No! He's ugly!" she screamed again. "I hate him!"

"A tornado has been sighted on Dort Highway!" the announcer said in an urgent voice.

That was across town from us.

"I repeat . . ."

"Turn him off!" Summer bellowed at me.

"No, Summer. Listen, listen . . ."

"If you are in the Dort Highway vicinity . . ."

"If you don't turn him off . . ." Summer hissed, and suddenly lunged at me.

Before I could react, she had smashed me over the head with the coffee cup. I was stunned with the blow. The cup shattered and the pieces went flying all over the room.

I touched my head gently and felt a stickiness in my hair.

At first I thought it was only Kool-Aid, but when I looked at my fingers they were covered with blood. I wobbled in my tracks. Summer just stood there glaring at me.

I wanted to throw up.

"And another tornado has been spotted on Corunna Road!" the announcer was saying.

That was closer to us. I can't be sick right now, I thought. And I can't think of my busted head. I'll have to worry about that later.

"We've got to get down into the basement," I said to Summer.

"No, there are wolves down there!" she screamed.

"Then do as you please!" I yelled back at her. "I'm goin' where it's safe!"

And I walked unsteadily into the kitchen and down the basement steps.

"*Nooo!*" she wailed miserably. "*Nooo! They* are down there. I won't go! *Nooo!*"

I heard a howling as I left my sister to fend for herself.

nineteen

Lucky for us, it was not a powerful tornado that swept down our street that day. It skipped around, hitting one house and missing another, almost like it was playing tag with us. I huddled in the basement in a daze. After the storm passed, I hurried upstairs and found Summer curled up in her bed with the covers over her head. She was not hurt.

Except for the swing set, which had been flung into the street, there was no damage to our place. Some of the houses near us had broken windows, and shingles and siding ripped off. Yard furniture was all over the place. But it could have been a whole lot worse, and we learned later that it was pretty bad in other parts of the city.

Henry came over to check on us about ten minutes after I came up from the basement. When I answered the door, he took one look at me and said, "Come on, girl, you're hurt. Let's git you to a doctor."

He took it for granted that I had been injured by the

storm. We couldn't get Summer out from under the covers, so we finally had to leave her there alone. I worried about her the whole time I was in the emergency room getting three stitches in my head. But when Henry took me back home, Summer was still in bed, where she stayed for the rest of the day and night.

Neither of us ever mentioned what she had done to me. But I told Poppy, and I watched his weathered face, strained from fear and worry, crumble into pieces.

"She's plum outa hand, Lyric," he said. "I don't see how we can hold on to her."

And I reckon we both recognized that it was time.

On a lovely day toward the end of August, me and Poppy dressed ourselves and Summer in our finest clothes, and keeping her firmly between us, we walked silently out to the bus stop.

When Poppy paused to tie his shoe, I felt Summer tugging at my sleeve and saying my name, "Lyric."

I turned to her. "Yeah? What is it, Summer?"

"Lyric, I'll be good," she whispered pitifully, and pleaded with her eyes. "I promise."

I looked into that anguished face, and it like to broke my heart. So she knew where we were going, I thought.

I put my arm around her. "Oh, Summer, you *are* good, you are as good as you *can* be!"

And it was the truth. She could no more control her behavior than she could fly away from the wolves. But the monster disease was in charge now, slowly but surely turning my once gentle, bright-eyed sister into a dark angry stranger.

We placed Summer between us on the long back seat of the bus to Pontiac, so that we could both hold on to her, but she was still as we drove through the green countryside.

It's funny how I remember little details of that trip. For instance, I remember the fragrance of some sweet wild bloom on a breeze from an open window. I knew I would never forget that aroma, and if I should ever smell it again, it would bring this moment back to me.

"Smell that?" I whispered to Summer.

Her eyes darted to my face, then Poppy's, but she didn't say anything.

I remember that the bus driver was whistling "Poor People of Paris." It was a real popular song that year. I had heard Poppy whistling it himself quite a lot, but right then his face was old and the saddest I had ever seen it. He did not feel like whistling.

I remember a young man and woman in front of us were sleeping with their heads together. Both snoring. I thought of what Summer had said that time about planning your tomorrows in your sleep. I figured those two were making their plans together and I couldn't help wondering if they ever dreamed the same dream.

I also remember arriving at the *place*, where a large friendly sign read *Welcome to Pontiac State Hospital*, like people might be entering these grounds to attend a party or something. I glanced at Summer to see if she had seen it. But she was leaning sideways and staring intently out the window up at the sky. I wondered what she saw up there.

We entered a huge red brick building where there was a man in the hallway barking like a dog. We steered Summer clear of him. There was also a woman pacing and jabbering nonsense words, just the way Summer was apt to do.

In a front office we were greeted by a young, pretty dark-haired nurse who Summer thought for sure was Jennifer Jones.

"I loved you in *The Song of Bernadette*," she gushed to the nurse, suddenly becoming very friendly. It was almost like she had found something solid to hang on to in deep water. "I'm going to be an actress, too. You will help me, won't you?"

"Yes," the nurse said. "I will."

"I can sing, too," Summer went on happily.

While Poppy signed some papers, I remember thinking how pleasant it would be for Summer to have someone she believed was Jennifer Jones to look after her.

I don't think Summer wanted to know where she was or even *who* she was. We said goodbye, and she didn't watch us walk away from her. She was busy talking to Jennifer Jones.

"I usta be big. Then my shadow left me. I am the Incredible Shrinking Man. The President is experimenting with a cure."

The nurse was smiling at her, and I could tell she was kind. We heard someone screaming far off down a dark corridor as we left, and me and Poppy looked at each other with terror and torment in our eyes.

So we took her there and left her with strangers 'cause we didn't know what else to do. And we went back home and started a strange new life, a life without Summer in it.

It was something of a relief not to have to worry about what to do with her all the time when we had to go here and we had to go there.

We didn't have to think about it anymore.

We could just go with an easy mind.

So we were free.

Still, we found it awful hard and painful to fill up that great big old gaping hole in our lives where Summer had been.

And sometimes in my sleep I could hear her whispering, "I'll be good, Lyric, I promise."

Oh, Summer, Summer, I had to let go!

A few days later when we arrived at the hospital for our first visit, Summer was curled up in a ball in her bed, the same way she had been that first day after coming home from Central High School. She wouldn't talk or even peek out at us. Just laid there she did, curled tight into herself.

Jennifer Jones told us Summer had had a bad reaction to one of her treatments. So we asked what did they do to her.

"ECT—it's electric shock therapy," Jennifer Jones answered matter-of-factly, like she was talking about aspirin or cough syrup. "It's a common treatment for schizophrenia, and usually very effective. But for some reason Summer reacted negatively."

Me and Poppy looked at each other in alarm.

"Electric shock?" Poppy said. "What do you mean?"

"It means we use electricity to disrupt the brain patterns."

"You shocked her brain?" Poppy cried out with a trembling in his voice.

"Well, yes, in a way . . . but what's wrong, Mr. Compton?"

Poppy had sunk to a chair beside Summer's bed and dropped his head on the bed beside hers. It was the only time I ever saw him cry.

Dr. Solomon seemed real smart and kind. We told him how scared of electricity Summer had always been, and he said they would not shock her anymore. He added that it didn't help her anyways.

By our next visit she had come out of her deep withdrawal, but we saw the real Summer only in little bits and pieces after that. And it was painfully clear to me that she really was disappearing. Even though the doctors and nurses were very good, they couldn't seem to bring our Summer back. I talked to Dr. Solomon again, and asked him if she was going to get better.

"We hope to take her home with us again someday," I said.

"I'll not lie to you, Lyric," Dr. Solomon said seriously. "You won't ever again see that pretty, vivacious teenager who *was* your sister. She is gone. I have never known a schizophrenic to recover completely."

He didn't have to say that. He didn't have to take away all of my hope. At least he could have said, "Hang on." So I didn't like Dr. Solomon after that, 'cause he was the man with the watch on, and he had told me the right time.

twenty

I read once that there is a purpose and a lesson even in bad things. I figured the main thing I had learned from what happened to Summer was to be more compassionate toward people who are different.

Like one day I helped a blind man cross the street, and he said, "God bless you, little girl." He couldn't see that I was all grown up.

Another time I saw a woman fall down, and I helped her back on her feet. I smelled liquor when I got close to her, but I went right on helping her, 'cause I felt compassion.

But surely God wouldn't let my sister go crazy just to teach me that! There had to be more to it. No, I figured there had to be something in this experience for everybody. I reckon Poppy learned a lot too. And the doctors and nurses learned more about mental illness.

And what of Summer herself? With her poor muddled mind like it was, it was real hard to tell if she had learned anything a'tall. But surely on some level she had to be the chief learner of us all, because wasn't she the chief sufferer? I didn't really understand all of it, this theory of everything happening for a purpose, but I had to believe it was true. Else, what was it all for?

On Labor Day the city was planning a street dance on the brick pavement downtown. They were advertising fireworks and carnival stuff. I dressed up pretty. I polished my fingernails with Summer's Precious Pink nail polish, and put on my matching lipstick. Then I went down there with Gladys, Nadine, and Yolanda.

Some boys flirted with us, and one of them asked me for my phone number. I just fluttered my eyelids at him, tossed my brown hair away from my face, and in my best Yankee accent I said, "I know you just wanna break my heart, Cutie Pie."

Gladys and Nadine and Yolanda looked at me with admiring eyes. I could tell they were thinking it was a feisty thing to say.

The wound in my heart hurt then. It was still fresh. Given time, I knew it would heal over, leaving only a thin blue scar. In fact, I had a brief vision of myself bumping into that tender place again in the middle of a dark winter's night somewhere in the misty future.

"Where'd you get that scar, Lyric?" I might ask myself then.

"That scar? Oh, when I was a little girl back in the hills, I had a beautiful sister, but . . ."

In our brightly colored summer dresses, we danced with the boys in the street. Laughing and whirling around and around, we were like fireflies, flitting and glowing in the summer dusk.

J   0003075
White, Ruth
Memories of Summer

OLD CHARLES TOWN LIBRARY
CHARLES TOWN, WV 25414

(304) 725-2208